T0147169

A Hebrew Understanding of the Difficult Passages in the Bible

Series One

Dr. Roy Blizzard Jr. Ph.D.

WestBow
PRESS®
A DIVISION OF THOMAS NELSON
& ZONDERVAN

WestBow Press books may be ordered through booksellers or by contacting:

WestBow Press
A Division of Thomas Nelson & Zondervan
1663 Liberty Drive
Bloomington, IN 47403
www.westbowpress.com
1 (866) 928-1240

ISBN: 978-1-9736-7638-6 (sc)
ISBN: 978-1-9736-7639-3 (e)

Printed in the United States of America.

WestBow Press rev. date: 10/01/2019

Contents

Foreword

As I look back over my life and consider where I am today, I have to acknowledge the contribution of two men, men who have influenced my life in ways that I will forever be appreciative of.

The first one, my late father-in-law, taught me the importance of reading and studying and digging into the word of God for myself. He taught me to question, to investigate and to search for opinions and answers other than those with which I had been educated during my formal years at University and Bible College, opinions and ideas which I had been predisposed to believe. I can remember him saying these words to me, as clearly as if it were yesterday, "What you have learned at Bible College you can write on the back side of a postage stamp," then pointing to his library he continued, "This is where you are going to get the knowledge you need to understand God's word." Those words set the course for my life 38 years ago and those words have guided me into a rich and wonderful relationship with God and a unique understanding of his word.

The second man to influence my life is a bible scholar and archeologist by the name of Dr. Roy Blizzard Jr., who challenged me to question everything I had been taught and to accept change when confronted with the truth, even when it went contrary to what I had been taught and defied what I believed. He taught me that it was arrogance that led me to believe that I "knew it all" and that it was narrow-minded foolishness that refused to change. I can remember him addressing a class, of which I was a part, and telling us that if we were not prepared to change what we believed, we were wasting our time studying and might just as well go home! What was the point of spending time studying in order to discover truth but being unwilling to accept what we discovered?

At the time I thought that this statement was rather conceited, not to say, offensive and I had it in mind to leave the class as soon as the session ended... but then he began to teach... and as he spoke and began to unfold the richness of understanding contained in the Hebrew text, I was fascinated and began to listen with intent. He continued to demonstrate to us just how much an understanding of Hebrew, not only the language but the context and the culture, could influence our understanding of the scriptures and forever change our perspective and religious worldview.

I had been a Christian for many, many years. I had risen through the ranks of traditional Christianity, had received a Bachelors degree, a Masters Degree and two diplomas and had ultimately been ordained as a Pastor in a mainstream denomination. As the morning progressed I realized that all of this was now 'on the line' and I began to realize the very difficult dilemma that was looming up before me. The very thought of questioning my entrenched beliefs seemed almost blasphemous and unacceptable but this new perspective with which I had now been confronted, was so overwhelmingly rational and enlightening that I could not ignore it. The predicament I faced was real and as I left that conference, I realized that I would be unable to continue without making a valiant and sincere effort to find the TRUTH. To find that truth which seemed to have eluded me for the better part of my life time.

I was forced to ask myself questions like this:

What did it benefit me if all that I could do was simply read the Bible without understanding what I was reading?

What did it help me to be so schooled in the sacred texts as to be able to quote verses, or even passages of scripture by heart, if I didn't know what those verses and passages really meant?

How could I teach God's word so convincingly so as to move men and women to tears and cause them to seek a change of lifestyle, if I didn't really understand what it was that I was teaching?

I remember telling my wife one Sunday morning as we walked out of church, "I am going to discover the truth, if it takes me the rest of my life to do so." That day I embarked upon a life of study which has changed my understanding of God's word forever. With the help of many, many scholars and the guidance of Dr. Roy Blizzard, I began to discover the unfathomable riches and yet, the beautiful simplicity of God's word as I began to explore the Hebrew text and understand the Hebrew context. How had I missed this? How come I'd never been taught this? The material I was reading had been available for years. The questions I was asking were rational and sensible so why had I never asked them before?

At first it was overwhelming. As I considered the vast amount of knowledge that was available to me and realized just how much of it I would have to familiarize myself with, I was tempted to throw in the towel right there and then. Then one day I came across these words of wisdom and they have been the inspiration that has kept me going over the years:

> "Learn in small doses. The little bit you learn, added to the little bit you know, makes just that little bit more."

> "How does one study Torah?" the Sages of old would ask, "One little verse at a time."

One day my wife informed me very clearly, "Not everyone likes to study!" Of course I realized that she was right, though the concept was a little difficult for me to grasp. How could someone not enjoying study and not be caught up in the thrill of discovering truth? I did realize however that some people just did not like to study. It was something that I had to come to grips with. To this end I began work on a book that I hoped would illustrate some of the easier to understand concepts of the Hebrew text. In it I set out to explain the basics of why it is so important to approach the scriptures from a Hebrew perspective and how just about anybody could do this if pointed in the right direction and given the right tools. I published the book, "Created in His Image, Kept by Covenant" but I really wanted to produce something simpler and easier to read. Then one day Dr. Roy Blizzard said to me,

"Why don't we collate some of the articles from the Yavo Digest and publish a book or series of books containing these easy to read, and informative articles?"

The idea was irresistible. Yavo Digest was a publication that Dr. Blizzard had published years ago on a monthly basis. In it he included wonderful articles explaining and expounding upon some of the difficult words that Jesus had spoken and explaining some of the difficult to understand texts in the Bible. What an opportunity to put into the hands of believers all over the world, some of the most fascinating and enlightening truths contained in God's word.

This publication and those that are to follow, "UNDERSTANDING THE DIFFICULT PASSAGES IN THE BIBLE", is the product of Dr. Blizzard's suggestion. I hope and pray that you not only enjoy reading these articles but that you will be blessed by them and inspired to continue to study and to seek for the truth.

Stewart Diesel-Reynolds M.A.

Author of:

"Created in His Image, Kept by Covenant"

Introduction

by Nehemia Gordon

A short while ago I found myself in Joplin, Missouri, in the living room of Dr Roy Blizzard, a man who is a genuine pioneer in the study of the Hebrew background of Jesus. I had been looking online at a website entitled *biblescholars.org*, just reading an article and minding my own business, when I noticed, at the top of the page, an invitation to come and study in a small group with him. I immediately thought to myself, "That can't be true. This is the man who wrote the book that I read years ago when I was exploring the Hebrew background of Yeshua," and here was an opportunity for me to sit down and study with the man who wrote the book!" Incredible! So, there I was.

Dr Roy Blizzard has a pretty impressive scholarly background. He has a BA from Phillips University with a major in religion. He has two different master's degrees; one in Archeology, Anthropology, and Religion from Eastern New Mexico University, and the other in Hebrew studies from University of Texas in Austin, Texas. Finally, he also has a PhD in Hebrew Studies at the University of Texas. He is the co-author of the book I alluded to earlier, the book which I read many years ago, entitled *Understanding the Difficult Words of Jesus*; a book which I consider to be a foundational book for anyone interested in understanding Jesus, or Yeshua, of Nazareth in his Hebrew and Jewish context. I cannot emphasize enough the significance of this book and the research that has gone into it. He has also written numerous other books, including one which is a virtual follow-on to *Understanding the Difficult Words of* Jesus, entitled, *Mishna and the Words of Jesus*. He really is a pioneer.

I was talking to my friend Keith Johnson about this and trying to explain to him what Dr Roy Blizzard and his colleagues did in trailblazing the study of the Jewish background of Jesus, and he came up with a wonderful and powerful analogy. He said, "You mean he's like Lewis and Clark?" Lewis and Clark had no idea what was west of the Mississippi, but they ventured on, bringing the Indian guide with them. Dr. Blizzard went to Israel and had his Jewish guides. Now you may say, "What's the big deal? He knows that Jesus was a Jew." This man *is* Lewis and Clark who blazed the trail that you are now walking on today, the trail that seems so easy. In the day that Dr Blizzard and his colleagues embarked upon this journey, back in 1966, it was revolutionary.

Dr. Blizzard had been the Pastor of a church in Oklahoma for thirteen years. One day, a young man who had previously been a member of his congregation, who was studying at the Hebrew University in Jerusalem, invited him to travel to Jerusalem and to study at the Hebrew University. Dr. Blizzard had just completed his master's degree at Eastern New Mexico University in anthropology and archeology when this young man extended the invitation to him. Lacking the resources to do this but stepping out in faith, he went to the bank and borrowed the money to go to Israel, and very soon after began his studies at Hebrew University in 1966.

As I sat in his living room talking and sharing stories about Israel, Dr. Blizzard made this incredible statement which I feel compelled to include here. He said the following:

"After being in Israel for a short while, meeting with, and studying under the leading scholars and archeologists in the land, I came to the realization that I could no longer continue to do what I was doing and be intellectually honest. All of the knowledge that I thought I had accumulated in the course of my studies, my supposed great intellect and learning, seemed to be insignificant in the light of what I had just been exposed to in Israel, studying under these scholars. I realized how little I really knew and how little I understood about all of this stuff. If I was going to be *intellectually* honest and honest to myself, I had to go back to school."

After returning to the United States and after extensive enquiry into different universities which had a Hebrew program, and with no promise of support or grant money, he eventually moved his family to Austin, Texas and enrolled himself in the University of Texas. There he became the administrative assistant to the chairman of the department of Hebrew studies, Aaron Bar Adon. At that time, Dr Blizzard told me, "I didn't know a Hebrew character from a 'chicken scratch' on the ground." Within 12 weeks of enrolling at the university, he was taking Hebrew courses presented by native Israelis, in the Hebrew language.

The year was 1968. In 1967, Israel had liberated the eastern half of Jerusalem, and one of the first things they did was to begin excavating around what we call the Western Wall. Dr Blizzard, now at the end of his first year at the University of Texas, was afforded the opportunity to go to Israel to work on the archeological excavation at the Temple Mount. The excavation was led by one of Professor Bar Adon's former colleagues, who happened to be one of the leading archeologists in Israel at the time, a Prof. Benjamin Mazar. Members of the Mazar family are still excavating in Israel to this day. At that time the Temple Mount happened to be the most impressive archeological excavation site in the whole of the country of Israel; everyone wanted to dig there. During the course of the 'dig', Dr Blizzard became good friends with Professor Mazar and in the years that were to follow, he would return to Israel, sometimes five times a year, to excavate on different archeological sites in the Land of Israel. He would even take students from the University on historical and archeological study seminars, where they would actually have the opportunity to excavate, or to be a part of an excavation, and to tour and study the different archeological sites.

In 1970 he was a part of the team which discovered and uncovered the historic Monumental Staircase leading up to the Temple Mount. In Jesus' day, when people walked up from the city of David into the Temple, they walked up these very steps. The Monumental Staircase was also the meeting place for all of the Jews during the three pilgrimage festivals, Passover, Shavuot (Pentecost) and Sukkot (Tabernacles). On these occasions they would gather on the steps in acknowledgement of the festival, to remember and reflect.

In addition to the monumental staircase, they also uncovered the "mikva'ot" or ritual immersion baths immediately adjacent to the Monumental Staircase, in which people would immerse themselves and cleanse themselves just as they were about to enter the temple. At the time of the discovery they were not aware of the significance of what they had just uncovered, but as the excavation progressed, they realized what these were. Now we can better understand the words of the apostle Peter in the Book of Acts, Chapter 2 and verse 38, when he says to all of those gathered there on the steps leading up to the Temple, "Repent and be baptized every one of you…." We now know that it was entirely possible for all of these pilgrims to have immersed themselves in a very short space of time because, adjacent to the steps upon which they were standing, was a whole immersion bath complex. Incidentally, in Hebrew the Temple is called, "ha-bayit" or "The House". When we read in the Book of Acts that they went 'up to the house', we know that they went up to the Temple, and from what we have learned about these pilgrimage festivals, they gathered on the steps leading up to the Temple; The Monumental Staircase. The Monumental Staircase is also significant for another reason: According to the Talmudic account, it was the place where a rabbinical court sat and proclaimed the calendar.

In my travels, I haven't met a lot of folks with a heavy Ozark accent who can quote to me from the Mishnah in Hebrew. Dr

Blizzard did. Referring to his book, *The Mishnah and the Words of Jesus,* I asked him why he thought that it was important for people to know what is written in the Mishna.

"First and foremost," he replied, "they need to know that Jesus was a Jew and as a Jew, he was acquainted with all of these rules and regulations; the different instructions that one finds in the Mishnah, and how that they were all passed on from one generation to the next. There are so many things that you learn in the Mishnah that relate to Jesus. For example, in the Mishnah, in Tractate Avot, it tells of a young man's education in Jesus' day. How he was being educated. That at five years of age he started his formal education. A lot of people were not aware of it, but you can go to Israel today, even until this very day, and talk to a parent and they will tell you that they start teaching their children how to recite the Psalms when they're as young as three years old."

I handed him my computer with Avot 5:21 open and he began to read: " 'Hu haya omer,' this is what he had to say: 'Ben chamesh shanim l'mikrah,' at five years of age, he's ready to start studying the scriptures, 'Ben eser l'mishna,' at 10 he's starting to study the Mishnah, 'Veben shlosh esreh l'mitzvot.' (Shlosh esreh) is thirteen, to the mitzvoth (the commandments).

WHAT DO YOU CALL YOURSELF?

I asked him this question: "When you go to Israel now and people see that you speak Hebrew and that you know about Jewish teachings, when they ask you, 'Ata Yehudi?', are you a Jew? What do you say to that?"

His answer was, " 'Ani omer lo' (I say no) - I tell them no. Their reaction is then, 'Well, you've got to be something,' and I say: 'Ani ma'amin. I am a believer.' And they say, 'What do you mean by that?' And I tell them, 'Ani pashut echad shma'amin beYeshua. Ve'ani mitkaven lilmod velenasot la'asot kol shehu oseh.' 'I'm one who believes in Yeshua and my intention is to learn and do everything that he says.'"

He continued, "The followers of Jesus, Yeshua, when describing who they were, used the term 'ma'amin', in English, 'believer'. Those who weren't Jews or weren't believers and who were opposed to them took a part of that phrase and as a slur called them, 'minim,' which is the last two syllables of believers, 'ma'aminim.' The term "Minim" means heretics. This was actually a curse on the Jewish followers of Yeshua that was established around the year 90 AD. Followers of Yeshua were not called Christians until much later. How much later we do not know but we read in Acts 11:26, *"And when he had found him, he brought him unto Antioch. And it came to pass, that a whole year they assembled themselves with the church, and taught much people. And the disciples were called Christians first in Antioch."* (KJV) Actually, they used the term, "meshichim" (messianics). 'Christian' was a much later term that was used.

WHAT LANGUAGE DID JESUS SPEAK?

Then I asked him the question: "Did Jesus speak Hebrew or Aramaic?" Here is his answer: "He spoke Hebrew, although he probably knew Aramaic and Greek. He may have even known some Latin. This is not just my opinion, it is just as clear here as it can be. It's often just overlooked because people do not know the languages well enough. But if you turn to Mark, I'll read to you what it says. In Mark chapter 15, verse 34, in English it says that *"in the last hour, the 9th hour, Jesus cried out with a loud voice saying, "Eloi, Eloi, lema sabachthani?"* Notice that it says, *"Being interpreted, my God, my God, why hast thou forsaken me?"* (KJV) In other words, that's not just in English. The phrase *'which is being interpreted'* is in the Greek text. In other words, what it is saying is that these words are being translated from some other language, and which language is it?

Well, let's examine what it says. In verse 35 we read *"And some of them that stood by, when they heard it said..."* and this is important,

"Behold, he calleth for Elijah." If you turn back to Matthew, in chapter 27, and verse number 46 it says, *"And in the 9ᵗʰ hour Jesus cried with a loud voice saying, 'Eli, Eli lama Sabachthani?' which is my God, my God, why has thou forsaken me?"* (KJV) It is important to note that in Aramaic, *"Eloi, Eloi,"* means only one thing, *"My God, my God."* It can never mean *"Eliyahu"* Elijah. The crowd, who understood Aramaic would never have interpreted *"Eloi"* as Elijah and they would never have concluded that he was calling upon Elijah. We must assume then that what they heard Jesus calling out was in fact "Eli, Eli, lama Sabachthani?" What is Eli? It means "My God," but it also sounds like *"Eliyahu"*, Elijah. It's a short form for *"Eliyahu"* and it is Hebrew. When the people said, *"Behold, he calleth for Elijah..."* it could only mean one thing: Jesus was speaking Hebrew, *"Eli, Eli"*, and the people who heard Him misunderstood and thought that he was calling upon Elijah.

"ONE CAN KEEP READING THE BIBLE FOREVER, AND THE BIBLE WILL NOT TELL HIM THE MEANING OF THESE DIFFICULT PASSAGES"

This is a powerful statement taken from the book *Understanding the Difficult Words of Jesus,* and I asked Dr Blizzard to explain to me what they (Dr Roy Blizzard and David Bevin)meant by this.

"Let me give you an example by way of explanation from Matthew chapter 6, verse 22," Dr Blizzard answered. "This is a verse that most of us have heard many times over, but I have come across few who really know what it means."

> *"The light of the body is the eye. And if therefore thine eye be single thy whole body is full of light."* (KJV)

"What does this mean? Some say it is 'single', some say 'whole', some say 'healthy', some say 'clear'. What is it? This is a Hebrew-ism and it's used even until today, as you know well. A good eye has nothing to do with vision. Look at the next verse."

"But if you've got an evil eye your whole body is filled with [choshech], darkness, and how great is that darkness." (KJV)

"When a Hebrew speaking person hears this verse in Hebrew, they have no doubt about what it means. 'Evil eye' means miserly or stingy, and a good eye means generous. These are just Hebrew expressions and the truth of the matter is that they are used many times in Mishna. 'Give with a good eye', means to give generously and 'with a bad eye' means that you give but you don't really want to; you're not really happy about giving. So, you can't really understand that phrase without understanding the Jewish context and the Hebrew context of that expression."

I asked him for another example, one I had heard him talk about before, Matthew 5:21-22. I had heard this one but, until I had heard him make the connections, I didn't get it. Afterwards it seemed obvious, but I don't know that I would've ever made the connection myself.

Here was his answer:

"You've heard that it was said by them of old time, thou shalt not kill. And whosoever shall kill shall be in danger of the judgment. But I say unto you that whosoever is angry with his brother without a cause shall be in danger of the judgment. And whosoever shall say to his brother, raca, shall be in danger of the council. And whoever shall say, thou fool, shall be in danger of hellfire." Matt 5:22 (KJV)

"I want to ask my readers now: 'How many have ever heard their pastor, or anyone else for that matter, ever preach or give a sermon, or exegesis, on this particular subject?' The answer to that question is, 'Probably very few.' Let me give some background here that will help us understand what is going on."

"In the first century in Judaism they had certain courts of law. They had the 'Beit Din,' which was the house of judgment, which was actually a congregational court. They also had additional courts that were called 'Sanhedrin.' You may be more familiar with the term Sanhedrin than with the term 'Beit Din.' They had a small 'Sanhedrin', and they had a large 'Sanhedrin'. The large 'Sanhedrin' sat in Jerusalem and consisted of 71 members. This verse says, "*But whosoever shall say to his brother "raca" shall be in danger of the Sanhedrin. But whosoever "yomar ata hana'val..."*" – (whoever says 'you are "*naval*") *shall be in danger of hell fire*". (KJV) I'm going to go to this book, *Everyman's Talmud*. And I'm going to open it to page three which has to do with the 'Doctrine of God'.

> Whether atheism in the sense of dogmatic denial of God's existence was accepted by anybody in Biblical times and Rabbinic times is doubtful. But both in the Bible and the Talmud, the concern was with the practical atheist who conducted his life as though he would never have to be accounted to for his deeds. In the Biblical literature the statement, there is no god, is made by the Na'val. In other words, a morally corrupt person who, while acknowledging the existence of a creator, refused to believe that he was at all interested in the action of his creatures. His counterpart in the Talmud is the Apiko'res, or the Epicurean, who likewise denies the fundamental principle of religion by his abominable conduct. The rabbis defined the atheist as one who affirms there is no judgment and no judge in the universe irrespective of his disbelief in the existence of God.

"The question is: How did we get from the words '*thou fool*' in Matt 5:22 to '*naval*'? Jesus is using a rabbinic teaching technique here called '*Remez*'. '*Remez*' is a way of teaching by which the teacher will hint back at something that his audience already knows. In this case Jesus hints back at Psalms 14:1, and Psalm 53:1: "*The fool has said in his heart there is no God. They are corrupt, they have done abominable* [works] *iniquity, there is none that doeth good.*" (KJV)

What it means, *na'val*, is this person is separated from God. He's not in any kind of relationship with God. He doesn't care about God. We would say today that he was an atheist but that's not the term that they were using. What they meant was that he was an individual who might have believed that there was a God but didn't believe that in any way he was responsible for his own actions. Now that we have established that, 'What was so wrong about saying this that you'd be in danger of hell fire?'

Well, the truth of the matter is, that by making that kind of a judgement you were questioning someone else's relationship with the creator of the universe. You're saying that they're lost – they're separated from God and only God Himself can make that judgement. By doing this or by saying this you are making yourself out to be God! That kind of blasphemy would result in one being 'cast out from among his people', in other words, being banished and probably stoned to death and your body cast into the valley of Gehenna."

I was so intrigued by my conversation with Dr Blizzard and could have spent hours more reading from the Hebrew text and listening to him expound these texts from his vast experience. But I could not leave without asking him the one question that is always on my mind. It had been brewing in my head since the first day we had sat in his living room and he had mentioned something about the pronunciation of names. Most people who know me know that the pronunciation of God's name is something that is very close to my heart and so I said to him, "Dr. Blizzard, you have a PhD in Hebrew studies, you have been studying these things for decades, you've got stacks of books; in your understanding, what is the correct pronunciation of the name of the God of Israel?"

He replied, "It's not *my* pronunciation, it's what the biblical text says. When Moses asked God: 'What do I tell the people when I go back there to Egypt, who was it who sent me, and He says, "*ehyeh asher ehyeh*", and he goes on to explain that it is Yehovah.

He then took his bible and, running his finger along the Hebrew text, proceeded to read from Exodus, Chapter 3 and verse 13, translating into English as he went.

"And God said unto Moses, "*ehyeh asher ehyeh*", I am that I am: and He said, Thus shalt thou say unto the children of Israel, "*Ehyeh*" has sent me unto you. 15) And God said moreover unto Moses, thus shalt thou say unto the children of Israel, "YEHOVAH ELOHI" God of your fathers, the God of Abraham, the God of Isaac and the God of Jacob has sent me unto you. THIS IS MY NAME FOREVER, and this is My memorial unto all generations." He added, "If I am reading correctly, this says, "YEHOVAH".

With that I concluded my interview with Dr. Blizzard, the author of the ground-breaking book, *Understanding the Difficult Words of Jesus*, and it was goodbye to Joplin, Missouri, and a great weekend spent with a great pioneer in the field of Hebrew studies, Dr. Roy Blizzard.

Gemilut Hasidim: The Fundamental Principle of Biblical Faith

By Dr. Roy Blizzard

Matthew 5:20 *"For I say unto you, that except your righteousness shall exceed the righteousness of the scribes and the Pharisees, you shall in no case enter into the kingdom of heaven."* (KJV)

In a day that we are being told that it is a believer's destiny to rule and to reign, to take dominion and to claim what is his by right of inheritance, it seems appropriate to ask the question : What is man's real responsibility towards God and towards his fellow man? The Jews had a word for it. It was not rule, reign, dominion, claim; it was the word *tzedakah*. We can safely say that *tzedakah* is the foundational principle upon which biblical faith is based. *Tzedakah* is frequently translated in English as *righteousness* or *charity*. In the King James Version of the New Testament, the Greek word *agape*, is frequently translated as charity.

In Judaism, charity was equated with righteousness, and it was a religious duty incumbent upon all men to provide for those in need. God, the giver of all good things, requires from His gifts a share for

1

the poor, the fatherless, the widow and the stranger. Deuteronomy 15:10,11:

> "*You shall surely give him (the poor) and thine heart shall not be grieved when thou givest unto him because that for this thing the Lord thy God shall bless you in all thy works and in all that thou puttest thy hand unto, for the poor shall never cease out of the land. Therefore, I command thee saying, thou shall open thy hand wide unto thy brother, to thy poor and to thy needy in thy land.*" (KJV)

In Judaism this concern for the poor and the needy extended to legislation regarding the corners of the field, the gleanings of the harvest, the forgotten sheaf, and growth of the seventh year as designated for the stranger, the fatherless and the widow. (Leviticus 19:9,10; 23:22; 24:19-21) Every year the second tithe was to remain in the land to take care of the stranger, the fatherless and the widow (Deuteronomy 24:22-29; 26:12ff).

Rabbi Akiva was once asked by Tinnius Rufus, "Why does your God, being the lover of the needy, not Himself provide for their support?" Akiva replied, "By *tzedakah*, wealth is to be made a means of salvation-God, the father of both the rich and the poor, wants the one to help the other and thus make the world a household of love" (Mishnah, Babba Batra 10a). Charity, in this context can be seen as an assessment of the rich in favor of the poor. However, the other and more important aspect of charity is righteousness. The helpless has a right to claim the help of his more fortunate brother. The cry of the needy is an appeal to human compassion to which the child of God must respond, lest God execute the judgement of the fatherless and the widow and punish those who remain deaf to this call of duty (Exodus 22:20).

Throughout the biblical text, there is the idea that the poor and the forsaken stand under the special protection and care of God, who loves the stranger and is the father of the fatherless and judge of the widows. (Deuteronomy 10:18; Psalm 68:6, 15) Proverbs 19:7, *"He that has pity upon the poor lends to the Lord."* (KJV) Proverbs 14:31, *"He that honors Him has mercy on the poor."* (KJV) Psalm 41:1, *"Blessed is he that considers the poor. The Lord will deliver him in time of trouble."* (KJV) The "righteous man" of Job 24:15, is the man who is eyes to the blind, feet to the lame, and father to the poor. The "virtuous woman" of Proverbs 31:1, is the one who "stretches out her hand to the poor and reaches forth her hand to the needy."

In the biblical perspective, charity is an obligation of man to his fellow man. One of the earliest rabbinic maxims recorded in the Mishnah is the statement of Simon the Just. Order Nezikin, Tractate Avot, Chapter 1, Mishnah 2, which states:

> Simon the Just was one of the last survivors of the Great Assembly. He used to say, "Upon three things is the world based, upon the torah, upon divine service (Temple worship), and upon the practice of charity."

In Order Zeraim, Tractate Peah, Chapter 1, Mishnah 1, we read,

> "These are the things which have no fixed measure [in other words, no minimum or maximum specified in the law], the corners of the field, the first fruits, the festival offerings [those brought on Passover, Pentecost and Tabernacles], charity and the study of Torah. These are the things the fruits of which a man enjoys in this world and the stock of which remains for him in the world to come, honoring ones father and mother, charity, making peace between man and his fellow man, but the study of Torah is equal to them all."

Notice that charity is mentioned here as a practice that affords satisfaction or results in enjoyment in this world. At the same time it is accounted as a virtue meritorious of reward in the world to come. In Mishnaic times, every community had a charity box, and offerings were received every Friday for food and clothing, as well as charity for the transient poor.

In Josephus' Antiquities of the Jews (in XX. 2.5), we read of Queen Helena of Mesopotamia who, during a great famine, brought shiploads of wheat and figs to aid the starving. Her son, Izates, sent great sums of money to the "foremost men of Jerusalem" to distribute among the people. This is the earliest historical evidence of the existence of a body of men at the head of a community who were in charge of relief to the poor. This is an interesting parallel to the condition that existed in the early church, recorded in Acts 6:1-6. These "foremost men" served in the function of charity wardens or collectors called *Gabba'ay Tzedakah*. That these men were held in the highest esteem can be seen from the Mishnah, Order Nashim, Tractate Kiddushin, Chapter 4, Mishnah 5, where we read that:

> "Anyone whose ancestor was a *gabba'ay tzedakah* was entitled to marry into the priestly stock, and that they were exempt from a search being made into their ancestral origin."

The *gabba'ay tzedakah* decided who was worthy to receive assistance. His reputation was so high that he was never called to account for his administration (Shabbat 118b, Babba Batra 9a-11a). Charity was regarded as a form of sacrifice offered to God on behalf of the poor. Therefore, it was stated that only worthy persons should receive *tzedakah*, but even more important, that givers of *tzedakah* should be of unblemished character, for charity has the character of sacrifice. A blemished sacrifice was an abomination to God. (Tosephta Babba Kamma 99 and Deuteronomy 23:19)

In the early centuries before and after the time of Jesus, a hospice, or public inn, known as *pandok* (from the Greek *pandokeion*), was built along the major roadways to offer food and shelter to the poor traveler and the homeless. In the Talmud, Berakot 58b, we read where "Hana bar Chanilai, in Babylon, had an inn with four doors open on all four sides to all passersby. Sixty bakers were kept busy baking bread in the daytime and sixty at night for the bashful poor who would not be seen begging bread by day." The ancient *pandok* became the communal inn in the Middle Ages for the feeding of the poor and the care of the sick.

`Maimonides ("Yad" Matnot Aniyim 10, 7 through 14), lists eight different ranks of givers of *tzedakah*:

1. He who aids the poor in supporting himself by advancing him money or by helping him learn a lucrative occupation;
2. He who gives charity without knowing who is the recipient and without the recipient knowing who is the giver;
3. He who gives in secret, casting the money into the houses of the poor who remain ignorant as to the name of their benefactor;
4. He who gives without knowing the recipient, although the recipient knows who is the giver;
5. He who gives before he is asked;
6. He who gives after he is asked;
7. He who gives inadequately but with good grace;
8. He who gives with bad grace.

Although *tzedakah* is the general word translated charity, there is, nonetheless, a Hebrew phrase which encompasses a wider range of kindness than does mere *tzedakah*. That is *gemilut hasidim*, the bestowal of loving kindness. "*Gemilut Hasidim* is the most comprehensive and fundamental of all Jewish virtues which encompasses the whole range of the duties of sympathetic consideration towards ones fellowman." (Encyclopedia Judaica, Volume 7, p. 374).

Gemilut Hasidim is the phrase used in all of the above mentioned quotes from Mishnah instead of the word *tzedakah*. Rabbi Simla'i (Sotah 14a) said:

> "The beginning and the end of Torah is *gemilut Hasidim*. How so? At the beginning, God clothed Adam and Eve (Genesis 10:21). At the end, He buried Moses (Deuteronomy 3:6)."

In Succah 49b the sages tell us that *gemilut Hasidim* is greater in three ways than *tzedakah*. One who performs *tzedakah* (commonly translated as charity) by: (1) giving money to the (2) living (3) poor. *Gemilut Hasidim*, on the other hand is performed (1) either with money or with one's person (such as by visiting the sick); (2) for the benefit of the poor or rich; (3) for both the living and the dead. And the highest form of it, called *gemilat hessed shel emet*, is true *gemilut Hasidim* in attending, or at least paying last respects, to the just-deceased, who cannot reciprocate.

Notice that *tzedakah* can be given only to the poor, whereas *gemilut Hasidim* can be given both to the rich and the poor alike. *Tzedakah* can be given only to the living, while *gemilut Hasidim* can be given both to the living and the dead. A gift given with a frown to a poor man may be *tzedakah*. The same amount given with a smile and a word of cheer raises the level to the level of *gemilut Hasidim*. *Gemilut hasidm* is regarded as one of the three outstanding distinguishing characteristics of the Jew to the extent that whosoever denies the duty of *gemilut Hasidim* denies the fundamental principle of Judaism (Eccles. R. 7:1). He is even suspected of being a non-Jew. Only he who practices it is fit to be a member of the Jewish people" (Yev. 79a).

In the light of all of the teaching circulating in Christendom today on ruling, reigning and dominion, I cannot help but wonder how much healthier and more spiritually mature the children of God would be would we but return to the basic principles and foundations of our faith and learn what it means to practice *tzedakah* and *gemilut Hasidim.*

Remember the words of Jesus, "Not everyone who says to me, 'Lord, Lord,' will be part of my kingdom, but the one who does the will of my father in heaven." How are we to recognize the true children of God - By their positions of authority, the number of members in their congregations, or the size of their buildings? Jesus said, "By their fruits you will know them."

Perhaps true biblical faith could only be expressed with the statement, "Only what you do, do you believe." Only what you do towards God and towards your fellow man identifies you as a true child of God. From the biblical perspective, there is no doubt that what one does for one's fellow man is of even greater importance than what one does towards God.

When Jesus was asked what was the greatest commandment of the law, his response was, *"You shall love the Lord your God with all your heart, and with all your soul and with all your strength. This is the first and great commandment. And the second is like it, you shall love your neighbor as yourself"* (Matthew 22:37-39). (NKJV)

It is interesting, and no doubt important, that about a century later, the great Rabbi Akiva, when asked the same question, offered the same response. In view of all of the many teachings of the rabbis on this subject and in the light of the many words of Jesus, it might do us all well to pause and to reflect on the question:

What is my real responsibility to God and to my fellow man?

Old Wine is Better!

By Brad Young, Ph.D

Luke 5:39 *"And no one having drunk old wine immediately desires new, for he says, The old is better."* (NKJV)

The passage from the Gospels which is titled "The Question about Fasting" in Luke 5:33-39 is by no means named properly. While it is true that Jesus is questioned concerning the additional fasts introduced to the Jewish liturgical calendar by John the Baptist and the Pharisees, Jesus does not answer the question directly.

SHOULD WE CONCENTRATE ON THE QUESTION OR ON THE ANSWER?

Perhaps this text has a deeper meaning. Why does Jesus respond and tell them that the bridegroom will be taken away? Why does he speak about a patch of new cloth in an old garment and new wine in old wineskins? Today, few people really understand these parables. In fact, the central point of the passage is often ignored entirely. This point emerges when Jesus says, *"The old wine is better"* (Luke 5:39). The fact is that fasting is not the major issue here. Although Jesus was asked about fasting, he wanted to say something more. He explained his own mission in terms that Jewish people of the first century could understand. When asked the question about fasting, Jesus took the opportunity to teach a deeper message. The message

8

of Jesus was intimately related to his task and to his desire for the people's salvation.

Is fasting the issue? Many bible students tend to ignore the final words of Jesus in Luke 5:39, *"And no one having drunk old wine, immediately desires new; for he says, 'The old is better.'"* (NKJV) The Jewish liturgical year included a number of specified fast days for the entire nation. On Yom Kippur, the Jewish Day of Atonement, all people afflicted themselves and fasted, asking for God's mercy and forgiveness. The Pharisees desired spiritual renewal. They wanted the people to be close to God all the time. Also the movement of John the Baptist was characterized by its urgency for spiritual revival. This bible passage indicates that both the Pharisees and John the Baptist instituted new fasts to intensify the spiritual awareness of the people.

WHAT DID JESUS THINK?

His disciples apparently did not observe these additional fasts. Jesus answers the question with two parables. The form of two parables is firmly rooted in the teaching of Jesus. Many Christians have ignored Luke 5:39 where Jesus tells that old wine is better and they have twisted the parables to fit modern times. They forget the reality of the life situation of Jesus and the Jewish world of the first century in which he operated. The old wine refers to the ancient faith and practices of the Jewish people. The question of fasting then related, not to the fast days of the accepted Jewish holy days, but rather to the special fasts of the Pharisees and the disciples of John the Baptist. These new fasts were called in addition to the accepted practice.

The purpose of Jesus was to revitalize the old wine. He did not teach that Judaism of his day should be abolished. He compared it to an old garment which needed repair or to old wineskins, which means that the spiritual state was not ideal but he did not desire to abolish the faith. He says that the old wine is better. The old wine is Judaism.

Jesus wanted to revitalize the faith. He wanted to see fresh wineskins for the old wine. The truth and grace of the ancient faith must be renewed for all the people. Men and women must embrace the ancient faith with their heart and receive God's salvation.

The old wine is good. It teaches the way of life according to the faith in the one and only God of ancient Israel. But the old wine needs new wineskins. Men and women of God must be renewed in order to hold old wine. Jesus points the people to the truth of God's love and grace on the basis of the best in the old wine. But fresh skins are required for the old wine.

In a penetrating study of these sayings of Jesus, David Flusser has understood this particular meaning of the words of Jesus. (David Flusser, "Do you prefer New Wine?" Immanuel 9, (1979), pp. 26ff.) While many New Testament scholars would deny the truth of Luke 5:39, "The old wine is better," Flusser has shown the clear authenticity of the saying in his careful study of the Gospels. Flusser notes the results of his work, "The best option of Jesus' opinion about Judaism in his days would probably have been, if Jesus had said: 'Fresh skins for old wine!"

JESUS DESIRED TO SEE NEW WINESKINS – i.e. A REVITALIZED PEOPLE – ENJOYING THE BEST OF THE OLD WINE

When we understand the work of R.L. Lindsey, the Gospel of Luke cannot be discounted as a late corruption of Marks earlier version. The saying "The old wine is better" (Luke 5:39) cannot be attributed to the later Church. Jesus was telling the people something about his purpose.

When it comes to wine, the rabbis, along with all knowledgeable wine connoisseurs, would agree with Jesus. Old wine is better than new wine. The rabbis related wine to the study of Torah. The more one studies the scriptures, the more proficient one will become. Knowledge of the scriptures will change an individual's life. The rabbis said, "One does not feel the taste of the wine at the beginning but the longer it grows old in the pitcher, the better it becomes, thus also the words of Torah: the longer they grow old in the body, the better they become" (Soferim15:6)

Jesus desired to see new wineskins – i.e., a revitalized people – enjoying the best of the old wine. The old wine is best. A spiritual renewal is needed. The new fasts may contribute something towards this goal, but the future of the renewal will be linked to Jesus and his disciples.

Jesus was not against the Judaism of his day. It is the old wine. He did not come to destroy the law but to fulfill it. He desired a revitalization of the faith: A renewed people spiritually prepared for the best of the old wine.

Jesus speaks, moreover, concerning the bridegroom. In fact, the whole passage surrounds the image of the bridegroom. Why do Jesus' disciples not fast? The bridegroom is with them. The day will come when the bridegroom is taken. In Hebrew, the term "taken," used in this context, is a euphemism clearly understood to refer to death.

A wedding is for the bridegroom, the occasion of supreme joy in Jewish thought and custom. Great joy is reserved for the wedding ceremony. The exact opposite is the case for a funeral. The grief expressed at a funeral is the supreme act of mourning. Jesus combines the two strongest emotions of men and women. Joy is for a wedding and mourning is for a funeral.

His purpose is to revitalize fresh skins for the best of the old wine, but he speaks also of his redemptive mission. He is the bridegroom! He brings joy, as the joy associated with the customs of a wedding. On the other hand, he also brings mourning.

When Jesus said, "But when the bridegroom is taken away from them," The people were probably puzzled. The word "*is taken away*" (In Hebrew *Lukach*; in Greek *aparthe*) was another way of saying, when he dies or when he is killed. Why must the bridegroom die? How can you relate the joy of a wedding to the death of the bridegroom? Jesus quite possibly alludes to Isaiah 53:8 where the same Hebrew word refers to the death of the suffering servant. In Isaiah 53:8 we read, "*He was taken away from* [rule] *prison and from judgement ... For he was eliminated* [cut off] *from the land of the living.*" (CEB)

Probably the Gospel passage, "The Question about Fasting," would be more properly named as a prophetic reference to Jesus' suffering. The bridegroom is here. He brings renewal. He is fulfilling his mission. The old wine is preserved for fresh wineskins but the day will come when the bridegroom will be taken. He will die. This also will be a part of his mission.

According to Jesus the old wine is best! Christians should be *for* Judaism. They must come to greater appreciation of the Jewish roots of Christianity.

Brad Young received his doctorate at the Hebrew University of Jerusalem in 1987. His dissertation, written under Professor David Flusser's supervision, was titled "The Parable as a Literary Genre in Rabbinic Literature and in the Gospels. This is now available in book form titled "Jesus and his Jewish Parables."

Linen and Wool

By Stewart Diesel-Reynolds

In Leviticus Chapter 19 and verse 19 God gives us an instruction which, on the surface, seems very confusing. "…Do not let a garment mingled of linen and woolen come upon thee." What does that mean?

LEVITICUS 19:19

"…Thou shalt not let thy cattle gender with a diverse kind: thou shalt not sow thy field with mingled seed: neither shalt a garment mingled of linen and woolen come upon thee." [KJV]

I had never really given this verse much consideration before, probably because it seemed to relate to some obscure Hebrew religious custom and partly because it is one of those verses that we just tend to read over without paying it much attention. One evening, one of the gentlemen in our Shabbat group asked me the question: "What does it mean? Should we not wear garments mingled with linen and woolen and how does that affect me today?" It was a fair question, actually it was a really good question but, of course, I did not know how to respond to him because I had no idea what this verse was referring to. When I inquired of those to whom I usually turn when I am faced with questions like this, I received an overwhelming, "I don't know," so I began to dig around a little and my initial take on this subject went something like this:

Firstly there are a few "could be's". One explanation could be that different threads or fabrics like linen and wool would react to wear and shrinkage in vastly different ways and combining them could lead to premature damaging of the cloth. This very practical reason could have greater spiritual meaning as we consider all of the possible meanings of this portion of scripture and we'll get to that as I share my thoughts with you in the course of this article.

The second "could be" is that it could very well be linked to superstition and paganism. Perhaps the combining of linen and wool had some more sinister significance than is apparent to us at first reading – perhaps it was linked to the warding off 'spirits' or perhaps providing some special power or invoking some special favor from a deity worshiped at that time. The same could be true of letting cattle gender with diverse kind and sowing mingled seed in one's field. Perhaps these practices were linked to the worship of some deity other than Yehovah. The truth is that if this is so, it is an explanation lost in antiquity but one which may have made perfect sense to the people of the time.

Then again, it could simply be a reference to common practice of the day in an agricultural setting. These might have been things that these rural people just knew not to do; you didn't mix linen with wool because of the danger of the fabric tearing under wear and with shrinkage; you didn't let your cattle gender with a diverse kind because it destroyed the integrity of the breed and you didn't sow your field with mingled seed because it made it difficult, if not impossible to harvest effectively. These people were farmers, perhaps these things were common knowledge to them and the writer was using them as an illustration for the point he was making in these chapters. It could be that these were things which were simply not done; the "then day" equivalent of our modern proverb, "You don't spit in the wind."

Each of these can be of spiritual significance once we understand the gist of what these few chapters in particular, are all about. Before I look at verse 19 in more depth, let me say this: "There are two ways that you could approach this verse (19). You could take these instructions literally or you could find some figurative or metaphoric meaning in what they have to say.

Now you might take these instructions literally just as the orthodox Jews and Hasidic Jews take the tenants of Deuteronomy Chapter 6 literally : "...and thou shalt bind them for a sign upon thine hand and they shall be as frontlets between thine eyes.", and it would probably do you no harm to do so, but personally, I don't believe that these verses were meant to be taken literally but to be interpreted figuratively. [This is my personal belief] I believe that binding the words of Torah "as a sign upon your hand" had something to do with remembering Torah during the day while you were working with your hands and keeping them "as frontlets between your eyes" meant that you did not lose sight of Torah (kept it in the forefront of your mind) throughout your day. In the same way, writing "them on the doorposts of your house" had something to do with remembering Torah every time you entered your home and every time you allowed a stranger into your home and writing them "on your gates" meant that you remembered God's commandments, his statutes and ordinances every time you left your home and walked out through your gates so that you would not be defiled by the world into which you were to enter.

Of one thing, I am reasonably certain. This statement, :...*neither shalt a garment mingled of linen and woolen come upon thee..."* does not stand alone. It is a classic Hebraism, telling a thing in two or three different ways to drive home the point. Although it dates way back before the time of the Rabbis and the development of their teaching techniques, this form of instruction is derivative of the instruction to be found in Deuteronomy 19:15:

> "One witness shall not rise up against a man for any iniquity, or for any sin, in any sin that he sinneth: at

*the mouth of two witnesses, or at the mouth of three
witnesses, shall a matter be established."* (ASV)

For this reason then, this portion of scripture must be read and
interpreted in the light of the other two examples as well. *"Thou shalt
not let thy cattle gender with a diverse kind: thou shalt not sow thy field
with mingled seed:"* Together they are telling us something.

I think that the explanation to understanding verse 19 lies
somewhere in the previous chapter. Remember that the Tenach
(Torah, Nevi'im, Ketuvum) [Torah, Prophets and Writings] were
only divided into chapters in about 1205 and so chapter 18 is very
much a part of chapter 19. Let's read some of what it says in chapter
18 as an introduction to understanding 19:19.

*"Defile not ye yourselves in any of these things: for in all these the
nations are defiled which I cast out before you: And the land is defiled:
therefore I do visit the iniquity thereof upon it, and the land itself
vomiteth out her inhabitants. You shall therefore keep my statutes and
my judgements, and shall not commit any of these abominations: neither
any of your own nation, nor any stranger that sojourneth among you:
For all these abominations have the men of the land done, which were
before you, and the land is defiled."* (Lev 18: 24-27) (KJV)

The references leading up to this statement are clearly references
to pagan practices but those following are just as applicable and
are warnings and instructions to stay away from pagan practices.
Yehovah commands us not to follow after the ways of this world but
to follow his commandments, statutes and ordinances. Then verse
2 of chapter 19:

"...ye shall be holy for I the Lord (YHWH) am holy." (KJV)

What does it mean to be holy? The Hebrew word here comes from
the root word "qadash" which means, 'to be, to make ceremonially
clean or morally clean'. It can also mean 'to dedicate or consecrate
oneself or to sanctify (set apart for a specific purpose) oneself'. In

short, it means to be different. A commandment to be different from those around you and to do it by obeying his commandments, statutes and ordinances and by not following after the ways of the people living in the lands you are to possess.

What was God telling the Israelites in these chapters? He was telling them not to follow after the ways of the pagan world into which they were to be plunged. These ways were totally opposed to the ways of Torah and (God) YHWH sets out clearly what we are and are not to do. It is about being different from the world around us. It is (God) YHWH telling us that his ways are totally opposed to those of the pagan world. It is (God) YHWH telling us that in no way, shape or form do we belong together or in any way united with the ways of the pagan world. [Here I imagine God saying: "Let me give you an illustration to which you can relate."]

It would be like a garment made of linen and wool – they don't belong together and the garment would eventually be destroyed because of it; it would be like letting your cattle gender with a diverse kind, the integrity and the purity of the breed would be defiled and the result would be half-breeds which would be good for nothing; it would be like sowing your fields with mingled seed and then trying to coordinate a harvest of plants which would mature at different times and which would affect the integrity of the other and be almost impossible to harvest without spoiling one of the crops.

I felt pretty sure that I had at least made some steps toward understanding this somewhat veiled instruction that God gave to the Israelites of old. Then, inspired by Dr. Brad Young's article entitled, "Old wine is better," I began pondering on the verses in Luke Chapter 5, verses 36-39:

> *"He told them a proverb also: No one puts a patch from a new garment on an old garment; if he does, he will both tear the new one, and the patch from the new one will not match the old garment. And no one pours new wine into old wineskins; if he does, the fresh wine will*

burst the skins and it will be spilled, and the skins will be ruined (destroyed).But the new wine must be put in fresh wineskins; And no one after drinking old wine immediately desires new wine, for he says, the old is good or better." [AMP Bible]

Jesus' habit was to teach using the techniques of the rabbis. Here again in the same vein as in the illustrations from Leviticus 19, Yeshua uses the rabbinic technique of telling two stories, parables or proverbs, in order to illustrate the same point, thereby emphasizing and reinforcing his message and driving home the point he is making.

Firstly he tells the proverb of the new patch of cloth used to patch an old garment, which sounds a lot like Leviticus 19:19. "No one puts a patch from a new garment on an old garment..." Incidentally, this is another of the rabbinic teaching methods that Yeshua used, it is called "remez" in Hebrew. It simply means that the teacher hints back at something which he knows his audience is familiar with. In this case, he hints back at Leviticus 19:19.

Secondly, he reinforces his message by telling another proverb. "You don't put new wine into old wineskins." If we didn't understand what he was talking about when he spoke about the "new patch on an old garment", this second proverb explains the point he is making much more clearly. The question is: "Do we, who do not see things from a Torah based, first century mindset, understand what Yeshua is saying?"

According to Dr. Brad Young, in this particular discourse, Yeshua was responding to the accusations of the scribes and the Pharisees who had questioned the fact that Yeshua's disciples did not comply with the practice of fasting followed by the disciples of John the Baptist. These practices, incidentally, were not commandments as set out in Torah but were 'additions' to the law, instituted by the Pharisees and by John. What? Additions to the "Law"? Yes, absolutely! Citing Deuteronomy 17:9-11 and acting on traditions which go all the way back to Moses and Jethro (Exodus 18:19-22), the scribes and the Pharisees took it upon themselves to interpret Torah and to institute laws which they believed would prevent the people from disobeying God's commandments, His ordinances and His statutes. Today we refer to these decrees of the scribes and Pharisees as "Takanot."

A brief word of explanation here:

These new laws are referred to as "Takanot" from the root Takanah - תקַן – meaning: to make straight; to affirm; make right; mend; repair; set in order; establish and confirm. It is, "A new enactment or decree fabricated on the basis that the oral law allows for the rabbis to do it." Deut 17:8-12

Here's what the Oral Law has to say in Mishnah, "Pirke Avot" – The Chapters of the Fathers

1.1 A. Moses received Torah at Sinai and handed it on to Joshua, Joshua to the elders, and elders to the prophets.

B. And the prophets handed it on to the men of the great assembly.

C. They said three things:

       1) Be prudent in judgement
       2) Raise up many disciples
       3) Make a fence for the Torah

In Yeshua's proverb, Torah is the "Old wine" and the old wine is good. There is no reason to add to it or pollute it with new ideas. Torah is given by (God) YHVH and is sufficient in and of itself to direct our lives in a way which will lead to successful living; as Yeshua referred to it, living in the 'Kingdom of God'. Trying to apply some new law or to adopt some new tradition as law will only lead to the erosion of its values and will take away from the blessings of living a life of obedience to Torah. New ideas, like a new patch on an old garment, will tear at the truth revealed in Torah and like the "new wine", would be distasteful when compared with the "old wine", that which is aged and matured. The point Yeshua is making here is that Torah should not be meddled with.

As I have already stated, these proverbs used by Yeshua in Luke 5:36-39, are remarkably similar to the instructions contained in Leviticus 19:19. Now, understanding Yeshua's use of these proverbs, I am more convinced that these instructions given in Leviticus, which at first reading seem strange and beyond our grasp, refer to Torah and the danger of Torah being polluted by the syncretic infusion from the pagan influences to which the Israelites were about to be subjected. This warning is also set out for us in Deuteronomy Chapter Seven.

> *When the Lord your God brings you into the land which you are entering to possess…And when the Lord your God gives them over to you, and you smite them; then you must utterly destroy them; you shall make no covenant with them, or show mercy to them. You shall not make marriages with them; your daughter you shall not give to his son, nor shall you take his daughter for your son. For they will turn away your sons from following Me, that they may serve other gods; so will the anger of the Lord be kindled against you, and He will destroy you quickly. But thus shall you deal with them: you shall break down their alters, and dash in pieces their pillars, and hew down their Asherim, and burn their graven Images with fire. For you are a holy and set apart people to the Lord your God and the*

Lord your God had chosen you to be a special people unto Himself, out of all the people of the earth. Deut. 7:1-6 [Amp]

The warning is simply this: Don't allow your sons or your daughters to intermarry with the sons and daughters of the inhabitants of the land. He uses the very familiar agrarian illustration which these people of the land who raised sheep and cattle, would recognize immediately. "If you wouldn't let your cattle gender with a diverse kind to protect the integrity of the breed; in the same way I instruct you to keep your sons and daughters from intermarrying with these pagan peoples." In order to keep something "holy", you need to keep it pure, set apart and dedicated to God.

"Thou shalt not sow thy field with mingled seed." Don't allow the teachings of the pagan nations around you to become integrated with the teachings of Torah. In fact, in Deuteronomy Chapter 7 we read that they are instructed to destroy everything to do with pagan worship – Break down their alters; dash in pieces their pillars, and hew down their Asherim, and burn their graven images with fire. Again, the illustration is something that these people of the land would relate to immediately.

Finally, linen and wool. *"Neither shall a garment mingled of linen and woollen come upon thee."* The emphasis here is on purity, separation and exclusivity as a means of protecting the integrity of, in the case of the proverb, the garment; and in the case of Israel, Torah and the worship of the One True God, Yehovah.

Are we then to refrain from waring garments made of mingled fibers of which there are many in our modern culture? No, that is not the point. What God is telling us to do is to keep Torah and to live according to His commandments, His statutes and His ordinances without allowing the eroding influences of other religions, other cultures and other peoples to change the way we are supposed to live as set out in Torah.

"The law of the Lord is perfect, restoring the (whole) person; the testimony of the Lord is sure, making wise the simple. The precepts of the Lord are right, rejoicing the heart; the commandment of the Lord is pure and bright, enlightening the eyes.; The (reverend) fear of the Lord is clean, enduring forever; the ordinances of the Lord are true, and righteous altogether." [AMP]

Stewart Diesel-Reynolds has a BA from the University of Stellenbosch, South Africa and a M.A. from Regent University, Virginia Beach, Virginia USA. He has been a long time student of Dr. Roy Blizzard and has recently authored a book entitled: Created in His Image, Kept by Covenant.

References

1. The Amplified Bible. Zondervan Bible Publishers, Grand Rapids, Michigan. 1964 Zondervan Publishing House
2. The Holy Bible Containing the Old and New Testaments. King James Version. Thomas Nelson Publishers, 1990.
3. Mishnah

Matthew Chapters 5 – 7
The Sermon on the Mount

By Dr Roy Blizzard

The Sermon on the Mount was not presented by Jesus in the way that we have it recorded in our bibles today.

The Sermon on the Mount, which happens to be recorded for us in Mathew chapter 5-7, is the longest of the recorded dialogues or words of Jesus. As you look at this material, what are some of the things that immediately strike you, some of the things that you consider to be the most significant or of most importance? We could say that it's important because it's the longest record of the words of Jesus or, it's important because of the nature of its teaching. Before we even begin to study this discourse, however, we need to take a close look at some of the things that, for want of a better understanding of first century Judaism, we've actually overlooked or, in some cases, never been taught.

First of all, it's almost 100% certain that this material was not communicated by Jesus in the manner in which we have it in Matthew 5-7. Reading the gospels we get the impression that all of this material was presented on one single occasion. On the surface this may seem to be heretical to you. Perhaps this is the first time that you've ever heard a statement like this. You may be thinking, "Do you mean to tell me that Jesus didn't say this?" No, that's not what I am saying. Jesus did say it, he said it all but not at one time and not in the exact way in which we have it presented to us. There is a reason for this. One of the most important things for us to understand about this material known as the Sermon on the Mount, is that Jesus, the one who is recorded to have said it all, was a Jew. He was not just any Jew, he was a Rabbi. There are certain facts about being a Rabbi in Jesus day that we have to consider as we dig into this material. Just briefly let me give you a thumbnail sketch on this subject as I set the stage for those of you who are not familiar with the first century Rabbi.

As a result of our current research and studies in Israel, we know a lot about this individual, the Rabbi. You might have noticed, as you read the Gospels, that Jesus was called a Rabbi. He was recognized by his peers as being a Rabbi. Lawyers called him Rabbi, Pharisees, Sadducees, members of the Sanhedrin, the rich young ruler, all referred to Jesus as Rabbi. Many others, as well, referred to Jesus as being a Rabbi, so it can be established, without a doubt, that he is recognized, by those of his day, as being a Rabbi.

What was a Rabbi? A Rabbi in Jesus' day was not the official functionary in the synagogue that we see developing much later on. The Rabbi of Jesus's day was what we might call an itinerant peripatetic preacher. He wandered from place to place much like the prophet of the Old Testament. We have an interesting quote from the Mishnah, which is the Oral Law of the Jews, in tractate known as Pirke Avot, or Chapters of the Fathers, in which it says,

> (1:4) Jose Ben Yoezer said, Let thy house be a meeting house for the wise, and sit amidst the dust of their feet and drink in their words with thirst."

What does that mean? That doesn't say a lot about the housekeeping abilities of the lady of the house does it? No, joking aside, it has nothing at all to do with her housekeeping abilities. Prof. Safrai, a professor at the Hebrew University in Jerusalem and one of the world's foremost scholars in Jewish history from the second temple period, points out that this passage in Hebrew means literally 'to cover yourself with the dust of their feet'. As we know from Jewish sources today, in Jesus' day there were hundreds and thousands of such peripatetic Rabbis who were going all over the country, from place to place, teaching and instructing the pupils. There were only dusty paths leading from one city to another and as they walked behind the Rabbi, following him from place to place, they got covered in dust. This was the Rabbi of Jesus' day.

We also know quite a lot about their teaching and instructional methods. In order to understand these teaching methods, you are going to have to understand the following:

Did you ever wonder what Jesus did as a young boy? Did you know that in the Biblical text there is a lot mentioned about his birth, but from then until the age of 12, nothing is recorded? There is also very little about his life from the age of 12 until the age of 30 - by the way, did you ever wonder why Jesus began his ministry at the age of 30? Why not 18? Why not 20? Why not 25? What was he doing all of this time? All of a sudden he appears on the scene at the age of 30 out of nowhere. What's he been doing? We know exactly what he was doing. He was doing what every other young boy of his age would have been doing. In the Mishnah, in Pirke Avot, the chapters of the fathers, in 5:21 it says, "...use to say at 5 years of age one is ready for the study of Torah, or the scripture. At the age of 10 one is fit for the study of Mishnah. (6 orders, 63 chapters) What had he been doing? He had been studying (memorizing) Torah and Mishnah.

In Jesus' day the Mishnah was communicated orally. It was not written down until 200 A.D. and every Rabbi had it all committed to memory. Also important to know is that Jesus' day it was recognized by the Rabbis as being on an equal par with the written law. In many places in the Gospels we see Jesus quoting from Mishnah.

In the opening Mishnah of Pirke Avot it says,

"....Moses received the law from Sinai and he handed it down to Joshua, and Joshua handed it down to the elders, and the elders handed it down to the prophets, and the prophets handed it down to the Men of the Great Assembly."

We have from this point on in this particular tractate just one Rabbi handing down the traditions from generation to generation, from one Rabbi to the next Rabbi, and on and on until this material was written down at the beginning of the second century and continuing on well into the 5th century, until all of the Rabbinic literature as we know it today, was ultimately collected. But the point that I want to stress here about this corpus of literature, known as the Oral Law, or Mishnah, is not only that it was considered by the Rabbis as being as authoritative as inspired and as binding as the written law and was given to Moses at Sinai, but that it was committed to memory by the Rabbis of Jesus' day. Jesus refers to it in just that manner many times.

One thing that is important to understand here is that in Jesus' day, although writing was highly developed, (1000's of years before Jesus) all of this writing was done by hand. They didn't have a printing press and things weren't put into codex or book form. It was all written on parchment (tanned animal skins), or papyrus, a very laborious and costly process and as a result they didn't have books like we have today.

[We have written documents that date back to 3500 B.C. But we have manuscripts of the Biblical text that date form 150 B.C. The Isaiah scroll, from Qumran, all 66 chapters perfectly legible even to this day was 150 years old when Jesus was born. The scroll that we have in our possession.]

So as they studied, they might have had only one document or no document at all and they simply had to memorize the information that was presented by the Rabbi, who himself had memorized the information and was communicating it to them orally. It's difficult for the Western mentality to understand this. It is foreign to us but this is how Torah and Mishnah were taught in Jesus' day. This still goes on in the Middle East to this day.

The memorization of vast quantities of materials was of utmost importance. As a matter of fact, one of my colleagues at the University of Texas, while I was teaching there, he was a specialist of Islamic literature, born in Bagdad and was an Israeli ambassador to the African state of Chad. He's now teaching at Carmel in one of the Universities there. He was a specialists in Islamic literature. He told me that he had an Arab acquaintance who was a story teller. This story teller had memorized vast quantities of materials to such a degree that he could read a poem of one thousand lines, once, or he could hear it read once, and recite it word for word without making a mistake. He had a slave girl who could hear it twice and do the same thing. I'm telling you this simply because it's difficult for us, with our Western mind to understand this oriental method of study and learning. It continues in the Middle East and in Israel to this day. Vast quantities of material is committed to memory. The Jewish child actually started his education well before he went off to school. It began in the home. The parents were admonished to teach these things to their children. In the Talmud (Oral law that was written down in the 5th century) we have vast chapters telling us how they had certain exercises in which they were able to teach infants the Hebrew alphabet. Do you believe that infants could actually learn the Hebrew alphabet and to begin to memorize the scriptures. By the age of three they already had vast portions of the biblical text committed to memory. If you find it hard to believe, you might find it harder to believe, that in two days working only a few hours a day, my daughter taught my 18 month old grandson the entire Hebrew alphabet.

He has his own library of books and has most of them committed to memory. The point is that in Jesus' day, even the average person had vast quantities of Rabbinic literature, Midrash, Mishnah, as well as the entire Bible committed to memory. The other side of the coin is that if all of that is true that's a serious indictment against our religious education program in our homes and in our schools.

Look at what was happening. At 5 years of age one is ready for the study of Torah. At the age of 10 one is fit for the study of Mishnah and at the age of 13, for Bar Mitzvah (the fulfillment of the commandments). Remember the ceremony called Bar Mitzvah, or Bat Mitzvah for the girls, at the age of 12. For the boys it's the age of 13. At the age of 13 he goes into this ceremony where the responsibilities of the law now fall upon his shoulders. So Bar Mitzvah literally means 'a son of the covenant'. Bat Mitzvah means 'a daughter of the covenant'.

> "At the age of 15 for the study of Talmud. At the age of 18 for marriage. At the age of 20 for pursuing a vocation. At the age of 30 for entering into one's full vigor."

It's interesting that the Bible tells us that Jesus always followed the law. He said, "I didn't come to destroy the law but to fulfill it." How did he fulfill it? He fulfilled it by becoming the embodiment of it. It says right here in the Mishnah that at the age of 30 a man is ready to move out in his full vigor, into the full vigor of his ministry. When we see him at the age of 30 moving out into the full vigor of his ministry we see him with all of this education behind him, education which began when he was 5 years old, stepping out into his calling.

Now let's get back to their teaching methods. From recent discoveries and from Talmudic literature, we know how these Rabbis taught. Unfortunately, none of us paid any attention to it before. So let's pay attention now: There are a number of things that we know: We know that Jesus was a Jew; we know that he was a Rabbi and as such he was using certain rabbinical methods of instruction and that this instruction was all in Hebrew. Let's stop there for a moment for this last statement cannot be overemphasized. Many of you who went off to Bible College or Seminary and you were probably taught that the New Testament was written in Greek and that Jesus spoke Aramaic. Today we know, and it can be proven so conclusively that there is no room for argument or discussion, that the language of Jesus was Hebrew and not Aramaic. He taught in Hebrew and the language of the common people in Judea was Hebrew and we know exactly why - Aramaic was on a descendency.

Aramaic was the language of the east and the north over in Babylon. During the time of the Babylonian captivity it was in its heyday. When the Jews were in Babylon they learned Aramaic but something happened in 163 B.C. that led to a change in all of that. No-one has paid a lot of attention to this.

Question: What happened in Jerusalem as a result of a man by the name of Judas Maccabee?

Answer: The Maccabean revolt!

Between 167 and 160 BCE the Jewish revolt against the Seleucid Empire succeeded in regaining control of and subsequently cleansing the Temple, after it had been desecrated by Antiochus Epiphanes. This feast that is referred to in New Testament as The Feast of Dedication, we remember today as Hanukkah, which is celebrated about the same time as Christmas because the particular time of year in which this event took place was around December 25. This led to a religious revival in Jerusalem that led, not just to the cleansing of the Temple but to the revival of their religion and also to a revival of the sacred language, Hebrew.

From that time onward 99.99% of all of the inscriptions that we find on Jewish coins, on sarcophagi, on burial ossuaries and on inscriptions of all kinds, are in Hebrew. All, except a few of the Dead Sea Scrolls are written in Hebrew. The language of the synoptic gospels and the language of Jesus was Hebrew. We know from recorded history, from writings that go all the way back to the end of the first century, that very shortly after the establishment of the church, maybe as early as four years after the establishment of the church, the life story of Jesus is written down in Hebrew by Matthew. We have early patristic statements along those lines. Quotes from Papias tell us that Matthew wrote down the words of Jesus in Hebrew. The original life story that comprised the material that is now contained in our synoptic gospels of Matthew, Mark and Luke and the first 15 chapters of the book of Acts, was written in the Hebrew language.

Not only was he teaching in Hebrew, as he taught he was teaching according to the prescribed rabbinic methods. Only recently have we discovered what those methods were. Something else very interesting happened as a result of these teaching methods. Only when you understand what I'm fixing to tell you will you understand why it happened. This material, this consistent story, this life story that contained all of the great themes of Jesus, was fragmented and cut up into all kinds of little pieces. Why? The reason was simple, because the teaching methods of the Rabbi in Jesus day necessitated it.

We have been talking about Oral Law and how it related to the written law. I have mentioned that Oral Law was considered to be on a par and a tradition with the written law, that it was considered by the Rabbis to be just as authoritative and just as inspired as the written law. In Oral Law there is what is called Haggadah and Halakah. Haggadah comes from the Hebrew root "Ngd" which means to draw out. Haggid means to tell. Haggadah could be best translated as legend or story-telling. Haggadah was the way in which the early peripatetic Rabbi, the itinerating Rabbi who went from place to place in Jesus day, taught. This included the great Biblical themes that were full of homily, simile, allegory, metaphor and parable. They included all of those great themes of the nature of God and about how man was to live before God and how man was to live before his fellow man. The people of Jesus' day loved Haggadah. They thrived on it. It was the food that fed their spiritual souls. The Rabbi who could elucidate, enunciate, illustrate and illuminate the nature of God and the will of God for his people and by so doing bring the people into a closer relationship with God, was dearly loved by the people, and they followed him everywhere that he went.

Do you remember when Jesus was walking along the shore of the Sea of Galilee and he saw Peter and James and John, and turning to them he said, "Come, follow me." What did that mean? In Hebrew he would have said, "Walk after me." Do you remember what I said a few moments ago about the peripatetic Rabbi and what Rabbi Jose Ben Yoezer said: "Let your house be a meeting house for the wise, the teachers, the Rabbis and sit at the dust of their feet." It doesn't mean to sit at the dust of their feet at all. Remember what we said about the Rabbi of Jesus day, always going from place to place. Back then they didn't have any paved roads. In many places when you walk across the country the soil was so fine that it was just like flour and when you stepped on it and it swirled around your feet like powder. The long and the short of it was that if you wanted to learn from the Rabbi, you had to follow him around wherever he went and in doing so you'd ultimately be covered in the dust scuffed up by his feet. So, as you can see, the phrase, "Follow me", is a Hebraism for becoming a disciple. Jesus says, "If you want to be my disciple, if you want to learn from me, you're going to have to follow after me." You're going to have to go from place to place wherever I go, following after me and learning from me.

These Rabbis that concentrated on Haggadah, that could bring men and women into an understanding of God's relationship with man and the relationship with their fellow man, were highly esteemed and the people gladly "ate from the dust of their feet", which is what this passage in the Mishnah literally says.

> "They ate from the dust of their feet. They clothed
> themselves with the dust of the Rabbi's feet."

Something happened after the destruction of the Temple in 70 AD. There was a shift from Haggadah to Halakah. As I mentioned to you a few moments ago, the word Halakah means 'to walk'. Halakah comes from that root (hlch) which means to walk or to go; literally, 'the way in which a person is to walk' and so subsequently, Halakah also means Law. [It should be pointed out at this point that there are numerous Hebrew words which are translated into the English word "law" resulting in all kinds of misinterpretations and a lot of confusion about 'The Law'] There has never been, (to my knowledge at the time that this article was written) a comprehensive treatment on the effect that the movement of Jesus of Nazareth had within the framework of Judaism of the first century. Let me say this and I want to say it clearly and emphatically so that you will all understand, Jesus' movement was a movement strictly within the framework of Judaism in the first century. It was a movement neither separated from Judaism nor apart from it. It was right at the heart and center of Judaism in Jesus' day and thousands and thousands of Jews embraced his message. It's a myth to say that the Jews did not accept Jesus. Who do you think these people were that accepted Jesus on the Day of Pentecost? A few days after another group of 5000 accepted him.

We know that by AD 66, when the Jewish revolt began in Jerusalem, that about one out of every three Jews in all of Palestine was a believer or a follower of Jesus of Nazareth. In Jerusalem alone there were from 50 to 60 thousand believers. We see this reflected in A.D. 50, in Acts 15 with the Jerusalem council as they gather together to discuss the matter with the elders of the church, saying: "What are we going to do with all of these non-Jews that are embracing the faith? Are we going to impose upon them all the restrictions of law which they (the Jews) were following?"

Why is all of this important? What does this have to do with 'Nuggets from the Sermon on the Mount?' I told you that this material was fragmented and that this was probably not the way that Jesus originally delivered it. Not all at one time and not all in one place. Today we know how he taught. It has been stated in the Talmud that none of the original sayings of any of the Rabbis have been preserved and have come down to us in their original form. Why? Because of the Haggadic method of instruction. Certainly these are his words but the Haggadist would take a certain theme and divide his presentation, or his sermon, into three points. You thought that was new didn't you? It's written in the Talmud that their discourse consisted of one-third Haggadah, one-third Halakah, and one-third parable. We can say today, almost with certainty that this is how Jesus taught. As we see in the gospels the most magnificently and best preserved picture of this wandering Rabbi of Jesus day. As a matter of fact there are more words of Jesus and what he had to say, preserved for us in our Synoptic Gospels, than those of any other Rabbi from any early historical period. So Jesus and the Synoptic Gospels form for us the most important corpus of material for understanding the teaching methods of the early wandering Rabbi.

Jesus would see an incident such as the woman who flipped her few coins into the treasury and he would say, "Amen" – which affirms that incident. He would affirm whatever took place with the Hebrew term "Amen" and then he would go ahead and give a discourse, closing by illustrating it with two parables. Why two parables? They used two parables because "out of the mouth of two witnesses is a thing established" - a typical rabbinic method of teaching. Now, because of the way the Rabbis would take these various themes and cut them up and then add their own little bits and pieces of information for their audience, this material became fragmented. We have a very clear indication of this whenever we read in the first chapter of Luke. As he writes to Theophilus he says,

> "...for as much as many have taken in hand to set forth
> in order a declaration of those things which are most
> surely believed among us, even as they were delivered
> unto us...it seemed good to me also, having had perfect

understanding of all of these things, to write unto thee
in order..." (KJV)

Twice in these early verses Luke is saying that he is trying to take all of these things that have been fragmented and put them back into some kind of reasonable order. He wasn't the only one who had attempted it. That's the reason why, in the synoptic Gospels of Matthew, Mark and Luke, we have incidents presented in different order. For example, incidents 1, 2, 3, 4 in one gospel appear as 1, 3, 4, 5 in another. They don't follow the same order because they were fragmented and then reassembled by each of the writers of these gospels. The miracle of it all is that it's been preserved for us so magnificently.

Today, understanding how Jesus taught, understanding that the language was Hebrew and understanding the Rabbinic methods of teaching, we are able to go back and look at this material in a different way. We are able, now, to hear the words of Jesus and be illuminated by them in a more thrilling and dramatic and dynamic way than ever before. Now that we know the teaching method and how they arranged their material, we can take the material that we have and go back to the original, taking these words that are dismembered or separated and putting them back together in their original context. This is one of the most magnificent things that has been happening in the Jerusalem School of Synoptic Studies, they are working on the reconstruction of the original Hebrew gospel. When they're finished, it will be translated into English and will be accompanied by a commentary and we'll once again to be able to hear the words of Jesus in their original context and in the way in which they were originally spoken.

I have given you all this background information so that you will understand this that I am about to explain. This is going to help us to understand the Sermon on the Mount with much more clarity. The Rabbis used many methods of homiletical interpretation and presentation in their preaching and teaching. The principle one that

Jesus used is known in Hebrew as "remez" or hinting. Perhaps a better word for us to use in English is allusion. He's always alluding back to something with which his audience was familiar. It's only now that we understand that his hearers had all of this material memorized that we can fully understand this method of teaching. Do you remember - they had it all memorized? They knew the Biblical text by heart to such a degree that all the Rabbi in Jesus' day had to do was speak one word and the whole phrase, the whole sentence, the whole chapter, the whole book: A whole theology literally exploded in their minds and they knew exactly what the teacher was alluding to and what the message was that he was trying to convey. It was second nature to them. They understood exactly what was being taught because they knew and understood the scriptures and all of the commentary about those scriptures. Jesus used this method of teaching to great effect in his ministry.

If you've been to Israel and have visited the Mt. of Olives, if I were to mention the Mount of Olives to you, a whole picture would burst into your mind? You would see yourself standing there; you could picture the Kidron Valley and the third wall coming into the Temple compound. You would see the Hinnom Valley running into and joining with the Kidron Valley, the Temple compound and the silver Dome Mosque and the Mosque of Omar, the eastern wall of the Temple compound and the eastern gate that's been sealed up, and far off in the distance would be the Rockefeller Museum off to the north. All of these things explode into your mind as I mentioned just one little statement, the Mt. of Olives. You see how that could happen when Jesus mentioned one word or one phrase or one sentence. A whole theology would explode in the minds of his hearers and they would know exactly what he was speaking about. It's only when you know these things and understand them that you can begin to feast on this vast banquet table of spiritual food that is recorded in Matthew 5, so magnificent and yet so misunderstood. I am going to show you how an understanding of these rabbinic methods of instruction were used by Jesus and how, by applying them, we can clearly understand what he was saying.

On many occasions I have discussed the Beatitudes and so I'm not going to open with the Beatitudes at this time. Instead we're going to turn to Matthew 5 and look at a few very interesting passages of scripture, passages which have caused us all kinds problems in the past. In my next chapter I'll begin by explaining The Kingdom of Heaven [God].

The Kingdom of Heaven

By Dr Roy Blizzard

Matthew 5:3 *"Blessed are the poor in spirit for theirs is the kingdom of heaven."* (KJV)

By way of introduction to understanding The Kingdom and to understanding the material we have recorded for us in Matthew chapters 5-7, there are several things that are of the utmost importance that I must remind you of, namely:

1. Jesus was a Jew;
2. He was a Rabbi;
3. He was speaking Hebrew;
4. His hearers to whom he was speaking were Jews who, not only spoke Hebrew, but had committed the Hebrew Bible (The Old Testament) and much of the Rabbinic literature of his day that was communicated orally, to memory;
5. Jesus was a Rabbi and as a Rabbi was using a particular method of Rabbinical study for teaching that is well known to us today. The particular teaching style of Jesus we could call in Hebrew *"remez"* which means hinting or perhaps a better word would be allusion.

In Jesus day the Rabbis had developed certain teaching styles, certain means and methods of interpretation of scripture.

Rabbi Hillel, for example, who was a contemporary of Jesus, had proposed 7 different methods of interpretation, methods which we later divided into 32 different means and methods of interpreting scripture. Beyond that, in the early part of the first century, in Jesus day, the emphasis in speaking and instruction on the part of the wandering Rabbi, who would itinerate from place to place with his students or his disciples following after him, was a concentration on Haggadah. This comes from the Hebrew root which means to draw out. It means a telling or relating and showing the relationship of information through homily, simile, parable, metaphor and allegory.

The people of Jesus day loved Haggadah because it was Haggadah that defined God. It brought the people closer to God and closer to their fellow man. It was only after the destruction of the Temple and after the tremendous influence that the believing community of Jews had upon Judaism as a whole, that the Rabbis began to concentrate on Halakah as opposed to Haggadah. Halakah comes from the root (hlch) which means to walk or to go. Halakah means 'the way in which a person is to walk or to go', it is a concentration on the legal definition of what it means to be a Jew and how to live like a Jew. This, however, came after the time of Jesus. In Jesus' day the concentration of the Rabbi was on Haggadah, the nature of God, the great themes of God and the inspiration that would draw man to God and man to his fellow man.

One of the most expansive of the sermons of the great Haggadic Rabbis of the first century, in so far as content is concerned, is that which is recorded in Matthew chapters 5-7 that is known as the Sermon on the Mount. An interesting fact is that in the synoptic gospels we have recorded more words spoken by Jesus than by any other Rabbi of his day. Our synoptic gospels paint for us the best picture of this itinerant, wandering, peripatetic Haggadic Rabbi as he wandered from place to place throughout the country expounding the great themes of God and inspiring men with his students following after him, eagerly 'eating from the dust of his feet'.

I don't believe that any serious or definitive treatment of the material recorded in the Sermon on the Mount has ever been done and I doubt that such could ever be done because it is so magnificent and so pregnant with power and meaning. Last summer Mr. David Biven, the co-author of our book "Understanding the Difficult words of Jesus", and I set out to write a book on the Sermon on the Mount. After about three days we decided to confine it to the first 8 beatitudes (vs. 3-10). We wrote for two months, working for 12 to 16 hours a day and never really finished the second word of the first beatitude. It was over 60 published pages. It will be published in a work called "Jesus and his Rabbinic method of teaching."

As we look at the Sermon on the Mount and begin to look carefully at this material, a great and overriding theme or purpose becomes obviously clear, without knowledge of which the rest of it becomes unintelligible. What is the overriding theme of the Sermon on the Mount? Well, if we paid careful attention to verse 3, it would become apparent:

> "Blessed are the poor in spirit for theirs is the kingdom of heaven." (Matt 5:3) (KJV)

This is actually a terrible translation. We don't understand it and the emphasis is upon the word 'blessed'. We don't know what 'blessed' means; we don't know what 'poor in spirit' means and 'kingdom of heaven' is something out there out in the future. In order to understand all of the Sermon on the Mount and the rest of the material that is contained in chapters 5-7, we have to understand that the basic theme upon which Jesus is concentrating is this: Who are kingdom people and how are kingdom people supposed to live? That is the central, underlying theme of the entire Sermon on the Mount. Kingdom; what is Kingdom; who are kingdom people and how are kingdom people to live?

Now he's going to begin to set that stage for us, to paint that picture for us, to lay the foundation for us when he says, "Blessed".

This is a poor translation. In Hebrew the emphasis is not upon blessed but on something else. We literally spent hours and days of study and research trying to determine how to best translate this one word into English. We concluded that the best way to translate this into English is not blessed but happy. We can say that the first eight beatitudes could be defined as "happiness is." However, the emphasis is *not* upon happy. Here the emphasis is upon *"the poor in spirit"* who are happy. The question is: What does it mean to be *"poor in spirit"* and what about those who are *meek,* who *hunger and thirst after righteousness,* who are *merciful, pure in heart,* the *peacemakers* and those who are *persecuted for righteousness sake*? What do all these things mean? If we can't figure this out we have absolutely no way of understanding what Jesus is teaching here.

One of the principle characteristics of Hebrew prose and poetry is the use of parallelisms. Parallelisms simply means saying the same thing over again, in the same way, perhaps amplifying it a little bit and looking at it from a slightly different perspective but without changing the meaning. For example:

Psalm 18:2 *"The Lord is my rock, my fortress and my deliverer, my keen and firm strength in whom I will trust and take refuge, my shield and the horn of my salvation, my high tower."* (KJV)

It all means the same thing. In the same way all of these eight beatitudes are describing kingdom people; they essentially define them and they are all essentially synonymous. This is what kingdom people are like.

Before we go on let's take a few moments and talk about 'kingdom'. What is kingdom? First of all, kingdom in Hebrew and for the Rabbis, was not futuristic. Kingdom was now. Kingdom for the Rabbis and kingdom for Jesus was present tense, right now. This is the reason that he makes such statements as:

> *"Take no thought for your life, what you're going to eat
> or drink, not for your body what you're going to put
> on, for all of these things the Gentiles seek."* ... *"Take
> therefore, no thought for the morrow."* (KJV)

Everything that he says here in the Sermon on the Mount,
fits together like the individual pieces of a jigsaw puzzle to form a
magnificent picture of what it means to be 'kingdom'. Here's the
thing though, if you don't understand the basic theme and if you
don't understand it from a Hebrew perspective, you're going to
completely miss the absolute importance of this all. Let me say that
again:

> If you don't understand the basic theme and if you
> don't understand it from a Hebrew perspective,
> you're going to completely miss the absolute
> importance of this all.

Take for example the different terminology, Kingdom of Heaven
and Kingdom of God. Actually, in Hebrew it is the same thing.
Kingdom of God was simply the Greek way of saying it because they
didn't have any problems using the name God, but in Hebrew, even
to this day, they won't use the name of God. How many of you have
received letters from those who are Jewish and instead of writing
'God', they write G-D because they have an aversion to writing and
saying or using the name of God. They use a string of euphemisms
such as, "the place", or "the name (Hashem)", or "Adonai" for Lord
or Master. They use Kingdom of Heaven so as to avoid using the
word God. So Kingdom of Heaven and Kingdom of God is the same
thing and it's important to understand that it is not something out
there in the future - it's right now.

Then, to the Hebrew thinker, there can be no Kingdom without
a King. Way back in Exodus we read, *"And the Lord God (Yehovah
Elohim) will reign for ever and ever."* (KJV) Who is King? God is.

There can also be no King without a Kingdom. Who then are the kingdom? The kingdom are those over whom God, the king, is ruling. For Jesus, kingdom people were those who were his disciples and his followers. They were being ruled by God and they were demonstrating His rule in their lives.

Where is kingdom? *"The kingdom of God is in you."* (Luke 17:21) (KJV) What does *this* mean? If the kingdom of God is in you then this means 'kingdom' is 'now'. So the emphasis is on 'now'. The emphasis in Judaism is not on tomorrow it is on today, the 'now'. That's the reason why he says take no thought for tomorrow. This is so important for us to understand. We run around like little chickens with our heads cut off, majoring in minors and playing some kind of little game that we call church and we haven't got the foggiest idea as to what's going on and what we are supposed to be doing. This may come as a shock, but I'm just telling you what's written. The Jews and the rabbis believed kingdom to be in the now and believed the emphasis for God's people to be in the 'now'. In fact there is a passage in the Mishnah, in one of the orders called Moed, seasons, and it has to do with the feasts and the festivals. In one of the tractates in Moed called Haggigag, meaning feasts or festivals, there is a statement that goes like this:

> *"There are four classes of people for whom it would have been better had they not been born on the face of the earth.* (Only if you understand Hebrew does the full import of this come through) *Those who are always asking, "What's up above?"* (Wonder where Heaven's at? What's it going to be like? What's it going to be like when we get there? Are there pearly gates and gold streets? Mansions over there on the hilltop) *Those who are always asking, "What's down below?"* (Wonder where Hell is? Wonder what it's going to be like? Will it be literal fire? Are we going to have to spend all eternity in anguish with eternal,

everlasting suffering, or are the unrighteous going to be consumed? Who's down there?) *Those who are always asking, "What's out there in the future?"* (Basically this is idle and foolish speculation and undue concentration on something about which you are not ever going to know anything about until after it already happens.) And then there are *Those who are always living in the past.* (We don't do things that way. This is the way that it's been done for years and I don't think that now is any time for change. Do you remember the good old days?)

As far as I'm concerned the good old days are right now. I want you to know that I'm not interested in 'pie in the sky, by and by'. I'm hungry now. I'm not interested in mansions over there on the hilltop because I need some place to live now. I'm not interested in what hell's going to be like and if it's going to burn with fire or whether we're going to be consumed or whether we're going to suffer eternally because I'm not planning on going there. I'm not interested in whether it's going to be a pre-tribulation rapture or mid-tribulation rapture or whether we're going through the tribulation or any of that foolish nonsense. The thing that I'm interested in is, whether the child of God knows who he is and what he is and who it is that's in him. I'm interested in him knowing that today, as a member of the kingdom of God, he can live in power and authority and victory.

This is the message of the Sermon on the Mount. What is kingdom? Who are kingdom people and how are they supposed to live. Who does Jesus say Kingdom people are? They are *'the poor in spirit'*. They are *'those who mourn'*. They are *'the meek'*, *'those who hunger and thirst after righteousness'*. They are *'the merciful'*, *'the pure in heart'*, *'the peacemakers'* and *"those who are persecuted for righteousness sake'*. [By the way the Hebrew word does not mean persecuted in the sense that we understand it.]

If we are going to understand what all of these things mean we need to remember that Jesus, as the haggadic Rabbi, is using the rabbinic method of instruction called "*remez*", in which he's always alluding to passages that are well known to his hearers. When he uses these terms, the people recognize them and the message he intends to convey literally explodes in their minds, not just the passage and the chapter, but the whole theology surrounding them. They had studied these exhaustively, both from Torah and Mishnah and understood exactly what Jesus was alluding to.

By way of explanation let's take a brief look at what some of these words mean.

Poor in spirit. Not surprisingly, "*poor in spirit*" doesn't have anything to do with poverty. "*Meek*" doesn't have anything to do with meekness and "*Mourn*" doesn't have anything to do with being sorrowful. What he is doing here is he is referring to passages in the Hebrew Bible [Old Testament] that are pregnant with significance and meaning.

Poor in spirit refers to passages from the book of Psalms:

> Ps. 34:18 "*The Lord is near to those who have a broken heart, and saves such as have a contrite spirit.* [Who are crushed with sorrow for sin and are humbly and thoroughly penitent]." (NKJV)

> Ps. 51:15-17. "*Oh Lord open thou my lips and my mouth shall show forth thy praise, for thou desireth not sacrifice else I would give it. Thou delightest not in burnt offerings. The sacrifices of God are a broken spirit: a broken and contrite heart, O God, thou wilt not despise.*" (KJV)

Who are the "*poor in spirit*"? They are those who are sorry for their sin and are thoroughly penitent. We read this in Isaiah 66:2:

"But on this one will I look, even to him who is poor and of a contrite spirit, and trembleth at my word. (KJV) [this is the man to whom I will look he who is humble and of a broken or wounded spirit, and who trembles at my word and who reveres my commands]. *"*

Who are the *"poor in spirit"*? They are those who tremble at His word and revere His commands.

Isaiah 57:15. *"For thus saith the High and Holy one that inhabits eternity, whose name is holy, I dwell in the high and holy place with him also that is of a contrite and humble spirit."* (KJV)

Isaiah 66:2. *"But this is the man to whom I will look favorably: to the one who is humble and contrite in spirit.* (ISV) [Even him that is poor and crushed spirit."]

What does it mean to be poor in spirit? We know exactly what it means. It means one who is sorrowful for his sins, one who is of a contrite heart, who has repented of his sins and has turned to God, who loves his word and who keeps his commandments. That's what it means to be poor in spirit.

Who are the happy? Happy are those who have repented of their sins, who have received his cleansing and his infilling, who have turned to God, who love his word, and keep his commandments; not only are they happy, but these are the ones over whom God is ruling now. These are kingdom people.

Do you remember what we said about parallelisms earlier? Well here Jesus employs that technique in classic style. To emphasize the point he is making, he continues to present his audience with other synonymous scriptural references:

Matt 5:4 "...*blessed are they that mourn for they shall be comforted.*" (KJV)

What does it mean to mourn? It means the same thing as to be '*poor in spirit*'. It refers to those who are broken hearted, who have reached the end of their own human strength and they cry out to God in despair and in desperate desire for his salvation. If that's true, what does comfort mean? Blessed are the spiritual mourners for they shall be comforted. What does comfort mean?

Isaiah 51:3 "*For the Lord will comfort Zion; He will comfort all her waste places and he will make her wilderness like Eden and her desert like the garden of the Lord.*

Vs. 12 "*I, even I am He Who comforts you...*" (ESV)

This sounds a lot like Ezekiel 34:11 where God takes personal responsibility and accountability for rescuing (saving) His sheep (people).

"*For thus says the Lord God: Behold I, I Myself will search for My sheep and I will search them out...I will rescue them out of all the places where they have been scattered...*" (KJV)

Isaiah 66:13 "*As one whom his mother comforts so will I comfort you, you shall be comforted in Jerusalem*" (KJV)

Comfort, as you can see is a synonym for save. "Blessed are those who are crushed in their own human spirit and cry out to God in helplessness and despair because these are the people who God is saving." These are the people who make up his kingdom. These are those who make up the 'saved'.

Matt. 5:5 *"Blessed are the meek, for they shall inherit the earth."* (KJV)

What does meek mean? We know exactly what it means. Look at Psalm 37 and verses 10 and 11.

> Ps. 37:10, 11 *"Yet a little while and the wicked is no more. Yeah, thou shalt look well at his place and he is not, but the humble (*'meek' - Amp Bible*) shall inherit the land."*

Here it goes on to call them the *"righteous"*.

> v. 21 *"The wicked borroweth and payeth not again. But the righteous showeth mercy and gives."* (KJV)

> v. 25 *"I've been young and now am old. Yet, I have not seen the righteous forsaken not his descendants* [seed] *begging bread."* (NKJV)

What does all this mean? Who is going to inherit the land? I want this so seared in your consciousness that you will not forget it because it's crucial to your understanding of the Sermon on the Mount. What does it say in Matthew 5? *"Blessed are the meek for they shall inherit the earth"*; now look at Ps. 37:11, *"But the meek, or the humble, shall inherit the earth."* Look at v. 29, *"The righteous shall inherit the land and dwell in it forever."* See how all of these terms are synonymous? What does it mean to be meek? What does it mean to be poor in spirit, contrite in spirit, a spiritual mourner, meek? It means to be righteous. Those who are righteous continually hunger and thirst after righteousness.

Now the question is, "What's righteousness?" Righteousness in Hebrew is not holiness. There is a difference between righteousness and holiness. This is of the utmost importance. It has to do with what I told you earlier. The righteous give. The Hebrew word for righteous is *tzedakah*. A righteous person is called a *tzadik*. Holy, on the other hand is the Hebrew word *kadosh*. Did you ever hear of *kadosh*? *Bet Mik-dash* means the temple the place of holiness, the place where the 'holy' lives or dwells. In Hebrew only God is holy. Only God is *Kadosh*. A place can only be holy if God is there. A thing can only be holy if it belongs to God. A person can be holy but only because God is there.

What then is righteousness? In Hebrew righteousness has two meanings and is used in two ways. In the limited sense, righteousness means alms-giving. Keep that in mind because in Matthew 5-7 Jesus is going to have something to say about alms giving. He's going to have something to say about righteousness. In the broader sense, in the Hebrew Bible (O.T.), righteousness is used synonymously with the word salvation. Blessed are those who are hungering and thirsting after God's salvation because they are the ones that are going to be filled. Filled means they're going to get saved. They are the saved.

What does merciful mean? Before I go further, let me reiterate what the Sermon on the Mount is about? It is about Kingdom and Kingdom living and how those who are in the kingdom are to live.

> Prov. 28:13, *"He that covereth his transgressions shall not prosper, but whosoever confesseth and forsaketh his sins obtains mercy."* (KJV)

If you confess your sins you receive forgiveness. Isn't that what John tells us in 1 John 1:7-9?

> *"He that is faithful and just to confess his sins, God will be faithful and just to cleanse him of his sins and to forgive him of all unrighteousness."* (KJV)

What does it mean to be merciful? It means to be forgiving. Blessed are those who are forgiving because they, in turn, shall be forgiven. Keep that in mind because Jesus is going to have something to say about being angry with one's brother. Why is he mentioning all of this stuff? Why is he raising all of these issues? Do you see how it's all beginning to fit together, woven together like a magnificent tapestry?

Pure in heart. What does that mean to be pure in heart? This is a tough one:

> Ps. 24:4, "*Who shall ascend unto the hill of the Lord? Who shall stand in his holy place? He that hath clean hands and a pure heart. Who hath not lifted up his soul into vanity,* [who hast not taken my name in vain] *nor sworn deceitfully.* (KJV)

It means to be a man of integrity. It means to be a man or a woman of your word. It means to be an individual whose word is as good as their bond. It means to be an individual who does not lie, who does not use deception or deceit. It means a man or a woman who does not commit themselves beyond their means and then try to weasel out of their responsibilities. Do you remember one of the Ten Commandments is, "*Thou shalt not bear false witness* (lie)". In the sense in which it's used here it doesn't simply mean thou shalt not tell a lie. It means you shall not bear false witness which has to do with taking an oath and swearing to it in a court of law against another individual which is going to result in their harm, the underlying intent being that of deceit and deception.

There are many ways in which the body of Christ is being deceived today even by 'so-called' teachers and preachers of the word. They are deceiving people by means of false doctrine, deceiving them with error, deceiving them with spiritual bondage that is bringing them into bondage to a doctrine or denomination that is not allowing them freedom and liberty in the Lord. I believe that there is such a thing as spiritual deception by feeding the body of Christ on nothing more than theological pabulum and withholding from them the meat of the word. What does it mean to have a pure heart? It means to have refrained from lifting yourself up to falsehood and not to have sworn deceitfully.

Blessed are the peacemakers. What does that mean? What's the Hebrew word for peace? *Shalom.* Do you know what that means? The interesting thing about this is that you may only know one word in Hebrew, *Shalom,* but when you hear the word *shalom* you don't have to translate it. *Shalom* is *shalom,* but it's more than peace. One of my colleagues at the University of Texas, writing his Doctoral dissertation, wrote on the meaning of the Hebrew shin, lamed, mem, from which comes the Hebrew word *shalom.* It was 286 pages on the meaning of shin, lamed and mem. Shalom means wholeness, completeness, safety, security, to be at rest, to be whole and to be complete. This is important to understand because later on Jesus is going to have something else to say about it in the beatitudes.

What does it mean to be a peacemaker? Blessed are those who are bringing men into wholeness and into completeness and into peace and security that they might find rest, because these are the ones who are called the sons of God. That's what the sons of God are doing, they are bringing the body into wholeness, completeness, safeness, security, peace and rest.

> *"Blessed are those who are persecuted for righteousness sake for theirs is the kingdom of heaven."* (KJV)

There are four mistranslations in this passage alone. It has nothing at all to do with persecution. We do know exactly what it means because it is a direct quote from Isaiah 51:1:

"Harken unto me ye that pursue righteousness."

Remember that Jesus is alluding back to familiar passages and as he uses words like, poor in spirit, or meek, or mourner, or hungering and thirsting for righteousness, or pure in heart, the understanding of all of these passages explodes in the minds of his hearers. Here's the passage in Isaiah, *"Hearken unto me ye that pursue righteousness."* Now what does that mean? The next line tells us, *"Ye that seek the Lord."* See how it's a parallel structure? Pursue righteousness means 'to seek the Lord'. It just so happens that the Hebrew root *radak,* used in Isaiah 51 and in Matthew chapter 5, can be translated into English in two ways. It can be translated as either 'pursue' or 'persecuted'. The translators of our English text, when they translated this back in 1611, not knowing the Rabbinic method of teaching then and not knowing what we know today, used the word 'persecuted'. Back then it was popular to suffer persecution in hopes of attaining some kind of spiritual merit or reward. That's where this whole theology begins to develop; at a time when there was some kind of spiritual merit or spiritual reward to be gained by suffering for Jesus. However it is not so in rabbinic literature and is not so in the biblical text. This has nothing to do with persecution or suffering and should be correctly translated, "Those who are running after God's salvation are those that are happy."

Who are the happy? Those who have repented of their sins, who have turned to God, who love his word, who keep his commandments, who are broken in their spirit, who have a contrite spirit, who hunger and thirst after spiritual things, who are of a forgiving spirit, who are bringing people in wholeness and into salvation in the kingdom of God and who are actively running after God's salvation and the things of God and these people are happy. That is happiness in the truest sense of the word.

Thou shalt not kill

By Dr Roy Blizzard

Matthew 5: 21 *"You have heard that it was said by them of old time thou shalt not kill…"* (KJV)

In Matthew 5 we read this very interesting passage of scripture and I doubt, seriously, if any of you can tell me what it means. The first questions we need to ask in order to understand what is said here is: Who said this originally and where did they say it?

Well, we know where it was said because it was given to Moses on Mount Sanai when God gave him what we know as the Ten Commandments. We also know that it was not Moses who said it, but God. These are instructions which come from the 'heart' of God. This is recorded for us in Exodus 20:13, but what is God saying here? We need to know, right from the start, that this verse in the Hebrew text does not say what it says in the English translation, *"…thou shalt not kill."* As a matter of fact, almost all of the Ten Commandments have been incorrectly translated into English. It does not say *"thou shalt not kill"*. So what then does it say? All you have to do is go to any Hebrew lexicon and look up the root word, *"Reish, Tsadie, Ket"* and you'll discover that this word which has been translated in the general sense to mean *"kill"*, means something a little more specific in the Hebrew text. The Hebrew word *"retzak"*, in fact means 'pre-meditated murder'. It is totally different from and has nothing to do with justifiable homicide, i.e. homicide in the protection of one's person or in the protection of one's family or home, or killing in the defense of one's country. It has to do with pre-meditated murder. The instruction that Jesus is repeating here from the book of Exodus is, "You shall not commit premeditated murder." However, we cannot stop reading there because this teaching is not about 'not killing', or murder, it is about something else entirely. It is about how to live as 'kingdom subjects'. It is instruction on personal relationships in the kingdom of heaven, on a par with the instructions we find in Leviticus chapter 19. Jesus makes reference to Exodus 20:13 for a specific purpose. He is juxtaposing it with his next instruction, with what he is about to teach in order to give his next words more emphasis. We have said before that Jesus was a Rabbi and that he employed the rabbinic methods of instruction. Well, here he is doing just that. He is using a rabbinic method of teaching. Look at what he says:

> *"You've heard it said by them of old times you shall not commit pre-meditated murder..."* But he continues, *"I say unto you, that whoever is angry with his brother without a cause shall be in danger of the judgment. And whoever shall say to his brother "Raca" shall be in danger of the council, and whosoever shall say thou fool shall be in danger of hell fire."* (Blizzard)

What does all of this mean? Allow me to paraphrase:

> "You are all concerned about what is written of old about not committing murder, but let me bring to your attention some of the things that you need to be aware of, things that can ultimately *lead* to murder."

If every single word that Jesus had to say was important, we need to understand exactly what he is saying and also why he is saying it. It is because these things are so difficult for us to understand that we spend so little time reading in the gospels. A few months ago, while I was teaching, I asked this question: "How many of you, in your reading in the New Testament or in your teaching in the New Testament, concentrate most of your energy in the epistles as opposed to the Gospels? And then: "How many of you spend most of your time, almost exclusively, reading in the GOSPELS?" The response was convincing. Most of us devote most of our time and energy listening to Paul, who is trying to correct and set in order churches that are disorderly and factional, that are immoral and that are spiritually immature. The result is that most of our energy and most of our theology is based upon the words of Paul written to a bunch of poor, dumb Gentiles who didn't know anything about spiritual things and we've been neglecting the words of Jesus.

Just think of it and the seriousness of it for a moment. If the apostle Paul came to town and the Lord Jesus came to town and one was speaking at one place the other at another place on the same evening, if you had the choice of going to one or the other, but not both, where would you go? There wouldn't be any thought. It wouldn't be close. Paul would be over there listening to Jesus also. Why are we not devoting more of our energy reading in the gospels? It is because when we read this stuff in the Gospels, we don't understand it. At least when we read the Epistles, we think we understand them.

When we read stuff like this in the Gospels it's so difficult: What does He mean when He says?

> "I say unto you whosoever is angry with his brother...
> [Everyone who is angry with his brother without a
> cause] is duty bound, or obligated, to appear before
> the Bet Din, and whoever says to his brother "Raca"
> is going to be in danger of the council.; but whosoever

shall say to his brother thou fool shall be in danger of hell fire." (Paraphrased from KJV)

Firstly, what is the Bet Din? The Bet Din was a house of judgment. In Jesus' day there was a whole legal system that had evolved. There were several different kinds of Bet Din's. Jesus says, "*If anybody is angry with his brother he's obligated to go before the Bet Din.*" That's the lowest court and every synagogue had its own Bet Din. These are religious courts and are the reason why Paul told the Jews not to take these things to pagan courts. Thus we can see that Paul's instruction doesn't have anything to do with whether we enter into litigation with another or not. He is simply reminding them that they had their own courts, each of which had the authority to judge certain offences and that the Jews should use these courts instead of the gentile courts. Our churches aren't structured to deal with these matters in this way but back then, they were. Every community had its own religious court. When Paul said, "Don't take these things to the pagan courts", he was saying to the people, "Don't you know that you're supposed to judge these things in the Bet Din?"

"*...But whoever shall say to his brother "Raca" shall be in danger of the council* [he's obligated to go before the Sanhedrin]". (KJV)

The lower courts could judge in civil matters but it was only the Sanhedrin that could judge in civil and criminal matters. What does "*Raca*" mean? It means empty headed. It means that he hasn't got sense enough "to pound sand into a rat hole". It means he hasn't got sense enough to take care of his business. He's the type of person who is so empty headed that he can't be trusted and relied upon. He is the kind of person who doesn't know how to pay his bills and make payments on time. The long and the short of it is that if "*you say to your brother, Raca...*", it is essentially slander or liable and this offense could be judged only by the Sanhedrin.

"But whosoever shall say to his brother you're a fool ('naval')- shall be in danger of hellfire." [guilty of gehinnom.] (KJV)

What is a *Naval*? If we turn to Ps. 14:1 and Psalm 53:1, we find out exactly what this word *'naval'* or "fool" means and what Jesus is referring to. [Let me quote from the Amplified Bible]

"The [spiritually ignorant] fool has said in his heart, There is no God. They are corrupt, they have committed repulsive and unspeakable deeds, there is no-one who does good."

When He uses the word *'Naval'*, Jesus is using a term with which all of his hearers are familiar. They know exactly what he's talking about. They are very familiar with the psalm and they know what it implies. They know what the Bet Din is; they know what the Sanhedrin is; they know what a *Raca* is and they know what a *Naval* is. They know where these passages are located in the Biblical text and can recall them at a moment's notice.

Saying to your brother *"Naval"* or "You are the kind of fool who has said in his heart there is no God, you have dealt corruptly and have abominable iniquity and you do no good." It's stronger than simply saying that someone has no sense. You are in fact saying that "this is an abominably utterly corrupt person who does not know God." This may come as a surprise to you but when it says *"the fool has said in his heart there is no God"*, we think that that refers to an atheist. This is not a reference to atheism but refers to an offense much more serious. Do you know that in Jesus' day, in ancient days, in Biblical days, there probably wasn't such a thing as an atheist. It's only when we come to Madelyn Murray O'Hair and others, that we have such.

In Everyman's Talmud under "The Doctrine of God", p. 3, we read this:

"Whether atheism in the sense of the dogmatic denial of God's existence was accepted by anybody in Biblical and Rabbinic times is doubtful. But both in Bible and Talmud the concern is with the practical atheist who conducted his life as though he would never be held accountable for his deeds. In Biblical literature, the statement, "there is no God", is made by the naval. In other words, the morally corrupt person who, while acknowledging the existence of a creator, refused to believe that he was interested in the actions of his creature."

Do you see what's happening here? If someone is angry with his brother, he has to go before the Bet Din. If someone says that his brother is an empty headed fool then he has to go before the Sanhedrin, but if anyone says this person is morally corrupt, he's utterly worthless, he's a corrupt contemptable who does not know God. That individual is assuming the role of God in condemning that person to judgment and that is a position that is reserved only for God himself. Such a person who usurps the role and the position and the authority of God is in danger of Gehinnom or 'hell fire'.

In conclusion, why should Jesus spend time teaching the people that they were not permitted by Torah to commit premeditated murder when he was fully aware that they all knew this as a part of their lives, religion and very existence? Well, as we can see, he wasn't. He was teaching them something which he considered to be as important as the sixth Commandment, he was teaching them about living and having right relationships in the kingdom of heaven.

Committing adultery in your heart?

By Dr Roy Blizzard

Here is a scripture that few really understand and because of this fact, the body of Christ has been brought into unbelievable bondage.

> Matt 5:27 *"You have heard that it was said by them of old time you shall not commit adultery. But, I say unto you, that whosoever looketh upon a woman to lust after her has committed adultery with her already in his heart."* (KJV)

Firstly we need to ask two questions, both of which have the same answer: "Where was that said?" and "What was Jesus alluding to?" We know that he is alluding to the seventh commandment given to Moses at Mount Sinai but I wonder how many of us make this connection when we read Matthew chapter 5:27-28? Again we see Jesus making the connection between what he is about to say and an established *mitzvah* – commandment. He quotes from Ex. 20:14, *"Thou shalt not commit adultery,"* but then goes on to make this next statement: *"But, I say unto you, that whosoever looketh upon a woman to lust after her has committed adultery with her already in his heart."* (KJV) He does not stop there. He goes on to say, *"If your right eye offends you pluck it out, or if your right hand offends you cut it off."* My goodness! It is starting to get tougher and tougher to live in the kingdom.

I spent many years travelling around the country teaching on the subject of 'Marriage and the Family'. As a result of my appearances on television teaching on the subject, I have received literally hundreds of letters from people writing in with requests for further information on the subject or writing in asking questions about all kinds of problems they were having. One of the biggest problems with which these men and women are confronted, is lust. As a result, they confess that they've had all kinds of problems with this passage of scripture. It seems that they can't get the better of it. It's got a hold over them and they feel so condemned. They experience all of these feelings, thoughts and fantasies; they've gone through deliverance and they've tried everything that they can think of to try and get the better of it and yet it keeps on coming back over and over again.

I read an amusing book a number of years ago that was entitled, "A Funny Thing Happened on the Way to Heaven." In it the author was describing some of the events that had happened to him during his years of ministry. He described how one Sunday morning he had got up and preached a message on the Ten Commandments. He had spoken on the seventh commandment, "Thou shalt not commit adultery", the danger of it and the consequences it could have. After church, shortly after he had walked into his house, the phone rang. It was one of the elders of the church who was terribly upset. He informed the pastor that he had come under such conviction that he couldn't wait any longer. He had to call and confess that he had committed adultery 286 times, the most recent being just after the service was over that morning, as he was walking across the parking lot and had seen sister Jones...

In Matthew 5:28, does it not say that if you look on a woman to lust after her, you've committed adultery with her in your heart already? *This* is a big problem, isn't it? Actually, if you understood this scripture you'd see that this whole problem has been blown out of all proportion and if we had had just a little 'spiritual' sex education, there really would be no problem. We've so missed the boat in so far as the educational program of the church is concerned that there is absolutely no teaching in our churches, especially to our young people, on the subject of marriage; the family; what it means to be married; the responsibilities of marriage; what is expected of the wife; what is expected of the husband; what the whole thing is all about or what is the commitment of marriage. There is no discussion of the subject of sex. In fact we rarely even talk about it. We leave our children and our youth to come to all kinds of conclusions about sex, not from what they learn from the Biblical perspective or from Christian mothers and fathers, or even what they have learned from any kind of sex education program that we have presented in the church, but what they learn in school and 'in the gutter'. It's no wonder that there is a problem with it.

To add to the confusion we have all of these 'self-proclaimed' authorities on the subject, writing all of these silly little Christian books that are bringing people into further bondage. They have no background or training in the field of sex education, counseling or therapy, nor do they know anything about the Biblical text but they are making all of these pious pronouncements. I wish I had a dollar for every preacher and for every elder and for every deacon and for every teacher and for every man in the church who has come up to me and shared with me the burden they had of self-condemnation and guilt because of the lust that they couldn't get control of. Well now let's take a look at what it is that Jesus is saying about it. You see, I doubt whether anybody has ever explained to you what lust is and what it means to lust.

Let's look again at the passage I quoted from Matthew 5:28

> "You've heard it said by them of old time, thou shalt
> not commit adultery, but I say unto you that whosoever
> looketh (and that doesn't mean a casual glance) on a
> woman to lust after her, (lustfully, to possess her)..."
> (KJV)

There is a difference between the words that mean a casual glance and the Hebrew word "hamad", as used in Matthew 5:28. It says to look upon a woman to lust her. It doesn't say to lust for her or lust after her but to lust her. Such a person has committed adultery with her in his heart already. Now the key question is, "What does it mean to lust her?" I'm going to give you a direct quote from Brown Driver Briggs Hebrew lexicon on the meaning of the word "*hamad*":

> "Hamad means inordinate, ungoverned, (out of control), selfish desire of idolatrous tendencies."

It is where lust has reached such a point that it is out of control and the person has given themselves over in idolatry to possess that thing that is forbidden unto them. It has absolutely nothing to do with ordinary human sexual response!

Let's stop a minute and ask ourselves a question: Who invented sex? God did. Well, if He thought it up then it must be good because the Bible says that all that God does is good. He created the heavens and the earth and He said that it was good and everything that He did, He said that it was good. So if he thought it up then it has to be good and holy and it must be right and pure. He created us to be sexual beings. I don't know how many of you are aware of this but the sex drive is the strongest single emotion, or force, in the human body and mind, superseding even the desire for food on occasions. It all depends on how long it's been since you've eaten. The point is that it's natural for us to have sexual thoughts and fantasies just as long as they are governed and under control. It's part of our human emotional makeup. It was God given, God created and it's nothing to be embarrassed about or to be ashamed of. It's certainly nothing to be in condemnation for. Everybody has them, both men and women. There is only one class of individual that does not have sexual thought or fantasies - we call those liars.

What is the difference between an ordinary human response and the type of lust that Jesus is talking about in Matthew 5:28? Do we have any examples in the Biblical text? David and Bathsheba springs to mind. David walks out onto his balcony and just happens to see Bathsheba. This encounter sparks all of his natural human thoughts and emotions but then he allows those thoughts and emotions to get out of control and he begins to conspire to possess her at any cost and contrived upon putting her husband up on the front lines of battle so that he would be killed. This is when he moved from an ordinary sexual response into sin and lust. There is a big difference.

The Hebrew word *"lachmod"*, (Matt. 2:28 – from the root *"hamad"*), is selfish, ungoverned, inordinate desire of idolatrous tendencies. This may come as a surprise to you but it doesn't only have to do with things in the area of sex. You can lust after a car, a TV set, a watch or a diamond ring. You may like what you see in the shop window and may even desire to purchase the TV set or the diamond ring; there's nothing wrong with that. It's when you pick up a brick and throw it through the window to get it at any cost, that you move from window shopping into sin. Are you following?

Do not be condemned by your ordinary human, sexual response. You are a sexual being. God created you to be that. He created it for you to enjoy and to be fulfilled and happy. Live and enjoy what God created you to be, but…

"…if thy right eye offend thee, pluck it out, and cast it from thee…" (KJV)

What does it mean *"…if your right eye offend pluck it out?"* It simply means that whatever it is that is leading you into that ungoverned, uncontrolled, selfish desire of idolatrous tendencies - remove yourself from it. Abstain from the very appearance of evil. There is nothing wrong with normal sexual thoughts and emotions. It is when you allow those thoughts and emotions to cause you to fall into sin, into inordinate, ungoverned, (out of control), selfish desires of idolatrous tendencies that you have to take control. What does it mean to take control? You 'master it' (Gen 4:7). You exercise your God given ability to refrain from entering into unbridled, idolatrous activities and sin. Pluck it out simply means rid yourself of these things. It does not mean to gouge out your eye just because you looked at a woman and had a perfectly normal sexual and emotional response. If it did we'd either all be condemned to "hell" or blind!

Do Not Swear -
Do Not Take An Oath

BY Dr Roy Blizzard

Matthew 5:33-34 *"Again, you have heard that it hath been said by them of old time, Thou shalt not forswear thyself, but perform unto the Lord thine oaths. But I say to you, swear not at all..."* (KJV)

What is he saying here? Does it not say in Deuteronomy 10:20 that I am supposed to swear in His Name? At this point it would be good to remember what I shared with you in the chapter titled "Gemilut Hasidim - the Fundamental Principle of Biblical Faith" about what righteousness is and how we are going to be judged? Where do you think that Jesus got this material? Let's go back to Deut. 10:17 and read from there:

> *"For the Lord your God he is God of Gods and Lord of Lords, the great God, the mighty, the awful who rewardeth not persons nor taketh rewards. He doth execute justice for the fatherless and the widow and loveth the stranger in giving him food and raiment. Love ye therefore the stranger for ye were strangers in the land of Egypt. Thou shalt fear the Lord thy God.*

*Him shalt thou serve and to him shalt thou cleave and
by his name thou shalt swear."* (KJV)

Here it says that you're supposed to swear. Of course the word
swear doesn't mean cuss. It's impossible to cuss in Hebrew because
there aren't any cuss words in Hebrew. Hebrew is the only language
that doesn't have cuss words. If you want to curse you have to use
Arabic, which is very colorful, or German, English or some other
language but you can't do it in Hebrew. [Cussing, or the use of
vulgarity, is simply the feeble attempt on the part of the uneducated
mind to express itself forcefully.]

Swearing, in this context, refers to taking an oath that you're
going perform a certain deed or that you are not going to perform a
certain deed. This is a very common biblical principle. Righteousness
is defined existentially as the act of compliance with the terms of a
covenant and 'sin', the failure to comply with the terms of a covenant.

There are two words in Hebrew that are translated oath:
"*Shavah*" and "*Nedar*". How many of you have heard of Beer-Sheba?
Do you know why it was called this? In Genesis you will read that
there, Isaac came and he made an oath with a king of that particular
area and because of the oath that they had sworn together, they dug
a well and called it "The Well of the Oath", which translated into
Hebrew is Beer Sheva?

What does it mean that thou shalt not swear? At this point let's
go back to Matthew chapter 5.

> *"You shall not forswear but you shall perform unto
> the Lord thine oath. But I say swear not at all. Either
> by heaven, for its Gods throne, or by earth, for it's his
> footstool, neither by Jerusalem for it's the city of the
> great King, neither swear by the hair of your head
> because you can't make one hair black or white."*
> (KJV)

This part we've read, now let's read on:

> *"But let your communication be yea, yea and nay, nay*
> *for whatsoever is more than this becometh of evil."*
> (KJV)

I don't understand. What's he talking about? "Don't' swear and if you say more than yea, yea or nay, nay you become of evil?" How many of you have ever given this any consideration? How easy it is to make promises and then not keep them. How many times do we promise God that if He'll just get us out of a difficult situation then we would do this or that? If He didn't let this happen then we'd promise to do something. We make all kinds of promises to God and to other people and swear that we're going to do them. You know what I'm talking about without my elaborating and going into any great detail. What Jesus is saying here is, "don't be making rash promises, entering into oaths or covenants that you're not going to be able to keep."

On another occasion Jesus says,

> *"Not everyone that saith unto me Lord, Lord shall*
> *enter into the kingdom of heaven; but he that doeth the*
> *will of my Father who is in heaven."* (KJV)

Who is going to enter into the kingdom of heaven? He that doeth the will of God. On another occasion Jesus says: *"If you love me you're going to keep my commandments,"* and on another occasion he says, *"Whosoever heareth these saying of mine and doeth them I will liken them to a wise man who buildeth his house on a rock."* (KJV)

All of these passages are intricately woven together and have something to do one with the other. How does faith come? Faith comes by hearing the word of God and the word of God is His Law or his commandments. Jesus is saying don't be making all of these rash promises saying that you're going to do this and you're going to do that. What you do is when the word speaks you act and do it and when the word doesn't speak you don't act and don't do it. In other words, let the positive commands be affirmed with action and those that are negative commands be confirmed with inaction. Whatsoever I have commanded you to do, do it; and whatsoever I have commanded you not to do, don't do it. Anything that is more than this is not of faith but it is of evil. Why? Because it is less or more than what was commanded.

So it's not let your yea be yea and your nay be nay. It's, "know what the positive commandments of the Lord your God are and obey them and know what the negative commandments are and obey them." There are 613 written commandments of law some of which are positive commandments and some of which are negative commandments. They are negative when it says, "Thou shalt not" and positive when it says "Thou shalt". When it says "Thou shalt not", you don't do and when it says "Thou shalt", you do. Let the "Thou shalts" be done and the "Thou shalt nots" not be done. Anything that is more than this is evil.

The Measure With Which You Give

What does it really mean to hear the Word of God?

by Stewart Diesel-Reynolds M.A.

---

*"…with what measure you mete, it shall be measured
to you: and unto you that hear shall more be given…"*

How many times have we heard these words preached from the pulpit and how many times have they been used to urge us to give our money in an offering or towards some project or mission or to "sow" some financial seed with the expectation that God is going to "repay" us in abundance. The only problem with all of that is that this scripture has NOTHING at all to do with money or fiscal accumulation of any kind! If it has been used to urge you to give your money in the hope of getting a return, it has been misquoted and abused and the fullness and the blessing that this precious teaching of Yeshua is intended to convey, is in all its intents and purposes, lost to you. If you will give me just ten minutes of your time, I will do my best to enlighten you that you may both hear and understand exactly what Yeshua was teaching when he said:

> Mark 4:21-24 *"…Is a candle brought to be put under a bushel, or under a bed? and not to be set on a*

candlestick? For there is nothing hid, which shall not be manifested; neither was anything kept secret, but that it should come abroad. If any man have ears to hear, let him hear. And he said unto them, Take heed what ye hear: with what measure ye mete, it shall be measured to you: and unto you that hear shall more be given." [KJV]

The Parable

Vs 23 *"If any man has ears to hear, let him hear..."*

To understand what is being communicated here we need to project ourselves back to the first century and do our best to understand these words as they were spoken to a first century Jewish audience. These words were packed with meaning and significance for the people who were listening to Yeshua teaching. Most of this significance is lost to us, as we know little of the language and less about what was going on in first century Judaism.

Firstly, we need to take note of the fact that whenever we come across the repetition of words, like the repetition of the word "hear" in this verse, we can be sure that there is something really important that the speaker is trying to convey. There are a couple of things going on here; to fully understand what *is* going on we need to look at each of these independently.

First of all there is the play on words – "ears" and "hear" and the repetition of the word "hear". *"...He who has ears to hear, let him hear...."* Both of these are used essentially to achieve the same goal and so I will deal with both of them together. This form of literary style, the repetition of a word, describing or referring to an action in two different ways in the same sentence or linking a noun with a verb as above, "ear" and "hear", is common in the prose of the biblical narrative. It is used for emphasis or "to make a point" and the repetition serves to demand prompt and precise compliance to an injunction. It allows for no variance from the command and expresses the expectation, no, even the assurance, that the command will be carried out to the letter. This same form is used in Genesis 1:3

"And God said, 'Let there be light'; and there was light"

Here the writer repeats the words to show the precision and celerity with which the command was fulfilled. So too with the above quotation from Mark 4:23, ears are for hearing so let them effectively perform their task as intended by the Creator. There is, however, much more going on here than meets the eye: In Hebrew idiomatic language, "hearing" does not simply refer to passive listening, it also implies understanding and discernment. The Prophet Isaiah writes:

"You have seen many things, but have paid no attention; your ears are open, but you hear nothing." (KJV)

Also, in Matthew we read this,

"For this people's heart has become calloused; they hardly hear with their ears, and they have closed their eyes. Otherwise they might see with their eyes, hear with their ears, understand with their hearts and turn, and I would heal them." (KJV)

Clearly, hearing in this sense was not simply the auditory perception of sound, it implied hearing and discernment of what they had heard so that the message that was heard could be understood and could be acted upon.

This brings me to my second point. In Hebrew, "to hear" is "TO DO". In Deuteronomy Chapter 6 we have probably the most well-known and most often quoted portions of scripture from the Hebrew Bible (Old Testament).

"SHEMA" – "HEAR O Israel: The Lord (YHWH) our God is one (YHWH)."

Here I want to quote from; "Onkelos on the Torah: Understanding the Bible text. Deuteronomy." By Israel Drazin and Stanley M. Wagner. p.xx of the introduction:

> The first word, *shema*, is translated "hear." It is true that *"shema"* literally means "hear"; however, it should be obvious that God wants the Israelites to do more than to use their sense of hearing passively. The term "hear" is also a figure of speech for "accept" both in Hebrew and in English. When one says to another "hear me and do what I say," he means *"accept* my view and do what I am telling you." The command *"shema"* also has a figurative meaning: God wants the people not only to listen passively but to actively accept what He is about to say.

Also...

> Ex 24:7 *"Then he took the book of the covenant and read it aloud, so that the people could **hear**; and they responded, "Everything that Adonai has spoken, we will do and obey."* (CJB)

This statement by the writer of Mark, *"He who has ears to hear; let him hear",* (a statement which is repeated three times in The Gospel of Mark Chapter 4), is not a postscript to the previous verses, it is a reiteration of the essence of the message contained in those verses. So the first question should be, "What is the essence of the message contained in these verses of scripture?"

If you go back to verse one and read the chapter, you will discover that this entire discourse is about paying attention and comprehending what Torah is teaching. It is about KNOWLEDGE

OF TORAH and DISCERNMENT OF TRUTH. It is about how serious you are about "hearing" (studying; contemplating; thinking logically about and putting into practice) the commandments, the statutes and ordinances given to us by God in Torah. [I must add, at this point that it does not have anything to do with money nor does it have anything to do with the accumulation of physical riches by "sowing" or "giving" and expecting God to give it back to you in the measures with which you used in your giving. This is a misuse of this scripture by proponents of the so-called "Prosperity Gospel".]

Let's look at some of the illustrations used here in Mark Chapter four beginning with the parable of the candle. This story of the candle is a simple illustration drawn from a very common practice of the day, that of lighting a candle and setting it in some place where it will provide the best light for the household. This story might be what we, in the 21st century, call "a no-brainer". *Of course* no one would light a candle to produce light and then place it under a bushel (or a peck measure, a type of bucket used for measuring – mostly grain) or under a bed where it would serve no practical purpose and where it would produce no light for the household. When a candle was lit, it was placed in the most prominent place possible – on a lamp stand where it would best illuminate the household. The candle in this story is the Word (Torah) and the spiritual and intellectual illumination that comes from understanding the Word of God (Torah). The light it gives off is the influence that God's word has over the lives of those who "hear" discern the meaning of the Word and act upon it.

Your immediate reaction to this might be: "How can we possibly know and discern Torah? It is too confusing and too difficult to understand and, anyway, doesn't the New Testament do away with the "Old"? This reaction is simply because we have a totally different mindset from those believers who lived in the first century. We have not yet learned, what these believers, the audience to whom Yeshua was speaking, would take for granted. To them this was not at all confusing. They had (at least most of them) learned Torah by heart and could recite vast passages at the blink of an eye. At the very least, they would be able to recite all of the important passages and they would be able to bring these passages to mind whenever Yeshua, or any other teacher, made reference to them. In addition to this they would also be acquainted with the Oral Torah and would be familiar with the discussions, reasoning and teaching of all of the great sages regarding these portions of scripture.

When, for example, Yeshua used the phrase, "He who as ears to hear, let him hear", they would know immediately which portions of Torah he was alluding to and all of these verses and the teachings surrounding these verses would come flooding back into their minds and they would immediately understand exactly what the teacher was saying. This form of rabbinic teaching was called "*remez*" – a hinting at something with which their audience was already familiar. Here is one of the first portions of scripture which would have come flooding back to them when they heard Yeshua's words, "*he who has ears to hear, let him hear.*"

Deuteronomy 30:11-14.

> "*For this commandment which I command thee this day, it is not hidden from thee, neither is it far off. It is not in heaven, that thou shouldest say, Who shall go up for us to heaven, and bring it unto us, that we may hear (understand) it, and do it? Neither is it beyond the sea, that thou shouldest say, Who shall go over the sea for us, and bring it unto us, that we may hear (understand) it, and do it? But the word is very nigh unto thee, in thy mouth, and in thy heart, that thou mayest do it.*" [KJV] (Emphasis and amplification – mine)

They would have known that God has not given His Word in

such a way and in such language that it could not be understood and so that it could not illuminate the lives of all men on earth. He has not hidden it but has made it very public and very easy to understand. However to understand what these first century teachers were alluding to, you would have to know Torah. It needs to be "*in your mouth and in your heart so that you can do it.*" Unfortunately, most of us have probably only committed to memory the first line of "*Shema*" and perhaps John 3:16. When Paul writes to Timothy and tells him to "*Study to show yourself approved unto God...*" he is talking about reading and committing to memory, Torah. When you watch Jewish children doing their "study", what are they doing? They are committing Torah to memory so that it will be "*in their mouth and in their heart that they might do it.*"

When Yeshua criticizes and rebukes the Scribes and Pharisees, it is because they had over complicated the Word of God by adding to it a burden of man-made laws and traditions. These man-made laws are called - תקנות - "*takanot*" (*takanah sg.*) and are "enactments" or "reforms" issued by the rabbis which change biblical law. Traditions or - מעשים -"*ma'asim*", on the other hand, although also originating from the oral law, were integrated into Jewish society on the following basis: If a thing was done in a community for long enough and by sufficient amount of people, then it became – מנהג ישראל תורה היא – "*minhag yisrael torah hi*", which means simply "a custom of Israel is law.", thus, an act which was performed for long enough by sufficient number of people became a tradition which was to be obeyed by all. This practice evolved to the point where it multiplied and complicated the Torah to such an extent that it placed an unbearable burden upon the people of Israel and Yeshua preached vehemently against it. It was these reforms and traditions that were so difficult for the people to remember and conform to, that Yeshua was referring, not to Torah.

After the destruction of the Temple in 70 CE, especially during the 60 year period which ensued known as "*Yavneh*", the practice of issuing "decrees" was used as an attempt to redefine the system of worship for Israel in the context of the synagogue rather than the Temple, now that the center of Jewish worship and identity had been destroyed by the Romans. These man-made laws and traditions complicated the lives of the people to the extent that they obscured the Word of God and the people were now no longer concerned with Torah because they were consumed with the teachings of men. (Sounds a little like today!)

Jesus says, "No! The Word of God is like a candle set on a lamp stand." It *is* not and *should* not be difficult to understand, nor should it be too difficult to live by. He is of course hinting back at Deuteronomy chapter 30: 11-14 (above). Then He goes on to issue a warning: "But be careful! Watch out who you listen to. There are some who seek to lead you astray or not tell you the whole truth. Choose for yourselves reputable teachers – because what you let yourself believe is going to determine the destiny of your life from here on out." [My own words.] This could very well be a reference to the "teachings of men" i.e. the reforms and traditions which had begun long before Yavneh, but it has a very pertinent message which is timeless and which is very applicable today. "*Take heed*", be very careful and be selective when it comes to what you "*hear*" – i.e. What you hear and subsequently accept as truth so that you accept it and act upon it. This is going to determine the degree of success or failure in your future.

When Yeshua hints back to Deuteronomy chapter 30, those Jews who were listening to Him knew exactly what He was saying and exactly to what He was referring because they were well acquainted with what was written in the rest of this chapter. They had studied the book of Deuteronomy as children and could probably quote the entire chapter, if not the entire book, by heart without any difficulty whatsoever. They knew that this scripture did not end at verse 14 and that there were more verses to come with a message with which they too were familiar. They knew that it spoke of the danger of not knowing and doing God's Word. (This is where we, gentile believers or God-fearers are at a disadvantage, especially when reading the

"New Testament, because we are not familiar with the context in which these books were written and we don't "know" the scriptures to which reference is made. Thus we have to expend a little energy and time finding out these things if we are to understand what Jesus and the Apostles were talking about!)

This is what the Deuteronomy scripture goes on to say:

> Deut 30:15-19 *"See, I have set before thee this day life and good, and death and evil; In that I command thee this day to love the Lord thy God, to walk in his ways, and to keep his commandments and his statutes and his judgments, that thou mayest live and multiply: and the Lord thy God shall bless thee in the land whither thou goest to possess it. But if thine heart turn away, so that thou wilt not hear, but shalt be drawn away, and worship other gods, and serve them; I denounce unto you this day, that ye shall surely perish, and that ye shall not prolong your days upon the land, whither thou passest over Jordan to go to possess it. I call heaven and earth to record this day against you, that I have set before you life and death, blessing and cursing: therefore choose life, that both thou and thy seed may live:"* [KJV]

Don't these two scriptures sound familiar?

> *"Take heed what ye hear: with what measure ye mete, it shall be measured to you: and unto you that hear shall more be given."*

> *"I call heaven and earth to record this day against you, that I have set before you life and death, blessing and cursing: therefore choose life, that both thou and thy seed may live:"*

The amount of time and effort you put into what you study, committing scripture to memory, and what you allow yourself to hear, is going to determine the measure with which your blessings or curses are measured back to you.

The Amplified Bible says it this way: [They have got it right!]

> Mark 4:24 *"And He said to them, Be careful what you are hearing. The measure [of thought and study] you give [to the truth you hear] will be the measure [of virtue and knowledge] that comes back to you, and more [besides] will be given to you who hear."* [AMP]

You see, it is all about giving your time to "hearing" Torah. That is, to familiarizing yourself with Torah and committing it to memory so that it will be constantly before your eyes, *"...in your mouth and in your heart."* It is about comprehending what God is saying and then DOING it. It is about the degree of obedience to Torah which determines the extent to which you will be successful in life and in the Kingdom of God here on earth. It is about making choices. If you choose to obey His commandments, His statutes and His ordinances (Deuteronomy 28; 30:16) you will live a life that is *"tov"* (good) – we use the English translation "blessed" but *"tov"* so very much more than that. It means to be blessed, to be prosperous, to be obedient (to Torah and to live in the blessings which emanate from this obedience.)

Biblical "faith" is best explained by the Hebrew word - אמונה – *"emuwnah"*, which in essence means - steadfastness produced by having knowledge (of the Word of God). It is the acquisition of this knowledge which is of utmost importance to all believers, Jew and Gentile alike. It is the assimilation of this knowledge which is going to change us and enable us to grow. It is the assimilation of this knowledge, the knowledge of Torah, to which Yeshua is referring when He says,

> *"...with what measure you mete, it shall be measured to you: and unto you that hear shall more be given..."*

And it is this same assimilation of knowledge to which Paul is referring when he states in Romans 1:17 and Galatians 3:11:

> "*The righteous shall live by faith…*"

and to which the writer of Hebrews alludes:

> "*…but My righteousness one shall live by faith, and if he shrinks back, my soul has no pleasure in him.*"
> Hebrews 10:38

I would like to conclude with another few verses from the New Testament which you have all read many times. This is another portion of Scripture which 'hints back' at something in the Hebrew Bible – [*remez*]. Now that we have dealt with reference in the Hebrew Bible and you understand the "*remez*", let's see how much better you understand these next verses.

Amplified Bible

> James 1:22-25 "*But – obey the message; be doers of the Word and not merely listeners to it, betraying yourselves [into deception by reasoning contrary to the truth]. For if anyone only listens to the Word without obeying it and being a doer of it, he is like a man who looks carefully at his [own] natural face in a mirror; For he thoughtfully observes himself, then goes off and promptly forgets what he was like. But he who looks carefully into the faultless law, the [law] of liberty, and is faithful to it and perseveres into looking into it, being not a heedless listener who forgets, but an active doer [who obeys], he shall be blessed in his doing – in his life of obedience.*"

What Does it Mean
to be Born Again…

WHERE DOES THIS CONCEPT COME FROM?

By Dr. Roy Blizzard

John 3:3 *"Verily, verily I say unto thee, Except a man
be born again, he cannot see the kingdom of God."*
(KJV)

Where did Jesus get the concept of "born again?" Was it from Oral
Law, phases of the moon, or was it an entirely new concept? It seems
to me that this question about, "what it means to be "born again,"
causes the Church so much confusion that I think it is apt that I
deal with it here and now.

The truth of the matter is that Jesus' statement to Nicodemus
in John 3:3 had nothing whatsoever to do with the phases of the
moon, nor was it an entirely new concept in Jewish thought. This
is however, without doubt an idea that causes the "Church" much
confusion. By and large, the Church has never understood Jesus'
statement or even the whole question of salvation.

The question of salvation is not only one of interest, but one
which is imperative to our understanding of the biblical concept of
repentance, atonement and kingdom. As a matter of fact, one could
write a whole book on the subject. In attempting to produce a brief

answer to this, a most difficult question, I must point out to begin with that again the translators have got it wrong. Jesus did not say to Nicodemus, "*You must be born again.*" That is more of a commentary than a translation. What Jesus did say is this: "*You must be born from above.*" Understanding this makes all the difference.

In order to understand Jesus' words to Nicodemus, let's go back and ask ourselves, who was this man Nicodemus? What was his condition before God? What was it that he sought from Jesus? Nicodemus was not just any ordinary individual. He was a Pharisee, a spiritual leader of Israel, a teacher of the law, and he had sufficient spiritual insight to understand that Jesus was no ordinary man. When he came to Jesus by night, he came inquiring, not only as to who Jesus was, but, in a very real way, to find out how he could 'get in on the action'.

In order to understand Jesus' response, we must realize that for Jesus, THE KINGDOM OF GOD EXISTED THERE AND THEN, in the 'now', in the present and that it was centered in and around Him. When Nicodemus asks: "What must I do...?" (*essentially to get in on the action*), Jesus responds, "*If you want to be a part of My movement (i.e. Kingdom) you are going to have to have a change of heart.*"

Very important to understand here is that Nicodemus was not asking about salvation, salvation which would be, in essence, his guarantee that he would go to heaven when he passed on from this world. The issue here is not with the world to come at all. As a Pharisee, a spiritual leader of the Jews [as a Jew], he believed that he already had his part in the world to come. THE ISSUE HERE IS THE PRESENT. When Nicodemus had first come to Jesus, having seen the miracles happening, he was curious and was interested in finding out what it would take to get in on some of the action. His question was, "*What must I do to become part of your movement (to get in on the action)?*"

Jesus responds in a very rabbinic way. "*If you want to be part of my movement, you are going to have to be born from above – there is going to have to be a spiritual rebirth.*" In Judaism, this idea of spiritual rebirth is closely linked to the whole concept of "*teshuvah*" or repentance. Repentance in the sense of turning to God, being born anew by a change of heart.

This was a process that was intended to take place on a daily basis with the religious Jew, but centered especially in and around the Day of Atonement, the time for remembrance and repentance leading to forgiveness, a time of reconciliation and of right relationship with God.

In Jesus' day the Pharisees constituted the largest single body of religious leaders, the ones whose words and deeds basically set the course for the people to follow. Unfortunately there was also abuse of the law as certain of the Pharisees taught, as commandments, the traditions of men. In addition, they had also contrived all kinds of ways to circumvent their religious responsibilities. Many examples could be given and many other things said about the Pharisees.

We can only assume what kind of Pharisee Nicodemus was. Whatever might have been lacking in his life, at least he had spiritual insight and wisdom enough to come to Jesus but what is important here is Jesus' response, "*Verily, verily I say unto you, except a man be born of water and of the spirit, he cannot enter the kingdom of God.*" Be born of the water? This was, of course, a reference to the ritual immersion bath where Jesus believed that, upon immersion, one would experience a form of spiritual death in the laying off of sins and then arising from the water, would come forth into a new kind of life, being reborn or born anew.

For some in Jesus' day it was an event that took place on a daily basis. Nicodemus was very familiar with this concept but Jesus goes one step further and says to him, "*You must not only be born from the water of the mikveh,* (the ritual immersion bath) *but you must be born of the spirit, born anew, have a change of heart, a different sense of direction, if you desire to be part of my movement.*"

You see, again, the issue is not with "salvation," or getting to go to heaven, but with becoming part of Jesus' movement, the kingdom. Evidently Nicodemus did experience a change of heart for we read later on in the Gospels that he was one of the two, along with Joseph of Arimathaea, that came to Pilate to claim the body of Jesus to prepare it for burial.

It is most unfortunate that this whole subject has been misunderstood by the Church, for the result has been that, instead of seeing the Kingdom of God as a movement for today, a movement directed outward towards our fellowman, Christianity has basically become a movement with its primary focus upward toward God, looking to the future and to the day in which we can claim our eternal rewards. The result has been the lack of the sense of responsibility towards our fellowman and the increasing sociological problems confronting us; problems like world-hunger, homelessness, the elderly, the unemployed, widows and orphans etc.

It is time that the Church, the people of God, all men of good will who love God, lean once again to the words of Jesus. *"If you want to be a part of my movement, you are going to have to have a change of heart, a renewed sense of direction for your life."*

I might just add, in closing, as this affords me an excellent opportunity to do so, that this is one of the reasons why we undertook the project of attempting to re-institute in the consciousness of the people of God, the biblical concept of *tzedakah*, the idea that man is responsible to his fellowman, that we *are* our brother's keeper!

[Please see the article entitled, GEMILUT HASIDIM: THE FUNDAMENTAL PRINCIPLE OF BIBLICAL FAITH]

What is the Focus of Jesus' Teaching?

Dr. Roy Blizzard

Matthew 5:16, Jesus says, *"Let your light so shine before men that they might see your good works and glorify your father which is in heaven."* (KJV)

The focus of this study is: What was it that Jesus taught to His people? What was the focus of His teaching? On what subject did He dwell more than on any other? Did He in fact come to teach us how to worship God? Did He come to start a new religious movement? Why did He come? It is obvious that He did not come to start a church. He wasn't the founder of "The Christian Church", nor did He operate outside of the mainstream Judaism of His day. What was it that He, as the One who called Himself "The Son of Man" taught? (Dan 7:13-14).

In Matthew 5:16, Jesus says, *"Let your light so shine before men that they might see your good works and glorify God."* The question is: What does it mean to let your light shine before men? Does it mean that I go to regular worship services and that I offer up long lengthy prayers – that I know how to pray better than anyone else in the congregation or that I know how to sing or that I know how to praise God? Does it mean that I'm always there anytime they come together and that I tithe faithfully? What *does* it mean, "…that they might see your good works?"

The first thing to notice is that Jesus is emphasizing action! Remember that He is setting forth this principle upon which His movement is going to be built, when He says, "Suffer it (permit it to be so) for thus it behooves us to fulfill all *Tzedakah*, all righteousness. This word *Tzedakah* (righteousness) does not mean holiness! It has to do with, one's "anointing to judge", "to administer justice", "to administer truth", to "bring deliverance", "to bring healing" or "salvation".

In all of this Jesus says, *"Permit this because it is incumbent upon us that we go the whole way to complete Tzedakah."* *Tzedakah* is a word that we could probably never find enough words in English to correctly translate. Jesus comes up out of the water, the Holy Spirit descends upon Him and Jesus is presented by God to the world with the words, *"This is My beloved son, My anointed on whom I have placed My Spirit to reveal truth, obey Him."* We are told to obey Him and now He is telling us what it means to be ruled by God; what it means to be the one who manifests the rule of God in their life through action. These people are to be known as "The Kingdom." These are the ones who are to be a part of Jesus's movement. All the way through we note the emphasis is upon what those who comprise the Kingdom or who make up the Kingdom, are doing. *"Let your light so shine among men…"* How do I let my light shine? What does it mean? "That they might see your good works and glorify God."

Light dispels what? It dispels darkness. So, light can be manifest in practical ways, in many forms of action. I might dispel darkness by feeding the hungry. I might dispel darkness by clothing someone's who is naked. I might dispel darkness by ministering to someone's emotional needs. You can see how practical this all becomes.

"Think not that I have come to destroy the law or the prophets. I am come not to destroy but to fulfill. For verily I say unto you, until heaven and earth pass, one

jot or tittle shall in no wise pass away from the law until all be fulfilled. Whoever shall break one of the least of these commandments and teach men to do so, he shall be called least in the Kingdom of Heaven. But whosoever shall do and teach them, the same shall be called great in the Kingdom of Heaven." (KJV)

Notice again, *"...whosoever shall do..."* not just that they teach them, but that they do them as well.

For Jesus, "Kingdom" people are those who are demonstrating His rule in their lives with action

There are a number of things here that we need to stop and take note of. For example, *"...not one jot or tittle is going to pass from the law."* What law is He talking about? He is talking about Torah and what is Torah? Torah is the first five books of the Bible; Genesis, Exodus, Leviticus, Numbers and Deuteronomy. This is also called the Law or the Law of Moses. Talking about the Law, how many laws are there in Torah? There are 613. Now, you may ask, "How did they come up with that number?" The answer is simply this: When you look through the first five books of the Bible, every time it says "Thou shalt," it is considered to be a positive commandment and every time it says, "Thou shalt not," it is considered to be a negative commandment. When you add up all the positive commandments and all the negative commandments, the total comes to 613. These are also called the 613 *Mitzvot*. Jesus says that He so respects the *Mitzvot* that not one jot or tittle is going to pass until it is all fulfilled. In Hebrew it says, *"...there will not pass one yod or one kotz."* *Yod* is the smallest letter in the Hebrew alphabet. What about *kotz*? The scribes had a practice of decorating some of the letters with little decorative marks and sometimes they would put this little decorative mark on the *yod*. They did this to a number of letters. It had absolutely no meaning. It wasn't there for any other reason other than that they liked to do it. It was artistic and it didn't change the meaning of the letter or the word. This makes Jesus's statement all the more impactful. He says that His regard for the Law is so high that not one of the tiniest letters; not even one of the decorative marks on top of the letters was going to pass until it had all been established.

When Jesus says, *"I didn't come to destroy the law but to fulfill,"* what did He mean? How do you destroy the law? What does it mean, He didn't come to destroy the law?" Destroy really means 'to misinterpret'. To misinterpret it is to destroy it. To fulfill it is to correctly interpret it. So He says that His purpose in coming is to give by example a correct interpretation of the law. His regard for it is such that not one of the tiniest letters or even the decorative marks on the letters is going to pass away. Now the rest make more sense – *"And whoever shall break one of these commandments and teach men to do so, he shall be called least in the Kingdom of Heaven."* Whoever misinterprets and teaches men to misinterpret or misapply Torah, he is going to be least in the Kingdom, but whoever shall do and teach them, he'll be called great in the Kingdom.

Then He goes on to say, *"Unless your righteousness exceeds the righteousness of the scribes and the Pharisees you are going to in no wise enter the Kingdom."* Now here we've got this word righteousness, *Tzedakah*, again. Unless your *Tzedakah* exceed the *Tzedakah* of the scribes and the Pharisees, you're not going to be able to be a part of My movement, the Kingdom. It is important to remember that to Jesus Kingdom or "Kingdom people" are those who are ruled by God and who are demonstrating God's rule in their lives with action. Jesus sees Kingdom in a unique way gathered around Him, at which He is the heart and the center.

What does this statement, *"Unless your righteousness exceeds that of the scribes and the Pharisees...,"* mean? Does it mean that you are more holy than they are? Unfortunately we normally equate righteousness to holiness. In this context, righteousness doesn't have anything to do with holiness as we understand holiness. There are those who like to think of themselves as holiness people. Charismatics and Pentecostals have historically thought of themselves as being holiness people. However, in Hebrew, a thing, a person, or a place cannot be holy. Only God is holy. Holy is an attribute that belongs uniquely to God. The only reason why a person, a place or a thing could ever be deemed holy would be because God would be there. So, we are not holy. Only as He is in us and we become what He is. When He talks about this *Tzedakah* He is talking about righteousness in action or in performance. He says that unless your doing the law exceeds that which the scribes and the Pharisees are doing, you're not going to be a part of His movement, the Kingdom.

What was the focus of Jesus' teaching? It is summed up in one word, *"tzedakah."* Action! It refers to acts of righteousness now, in the present. It refers to loving helping your brother and *"loving your neighbor as yourself."* In fact, if you turn to Leviticus chapter 19, to which this verse points (remember *"remez"*), you will read exactly what you are supposed to be doing and how you are to treat your brother and you neighbor. All of this is in the "now". Not sometime in the future, not in the "sweet bye and bye". It is now.

To Jesus, Kingdom people were those who were doing the will of the Father, those who were acting out the word and doing! This was the focus of Jesus' teaching.

Questions and Answers

with Dr. Roy Blizzard

PHYSICIAN HEAL THYSELF

QUESTION: Dear Dr. Blizzard: In Luke 4:22-23, the people of Nazareth after hearing Jesus' words in the synagogue, asked, *"Is this not Joseph's son?"* And in verse 23, Jesus said, *"You will surely say unto me this proverb, 'Physician, heal thyself': Whatsoever we have heard done in Capernaum, do also here in thy country."* (KJV)

What does this mean? And where does one find the proverb, "Physician heal thyself"?

ANSWER: Reference to this particular passage can be found in the Eidersheim's Life and Times of Jesus the Messiah, on page 354, in the edition published by Associated Publishers and Authors, Inc. (Grand Rapids, Michigan.) Other editions will have different numbering of pages.

The reference is to Bereishis Rabbah 23. In Bereishis Rabbah 23 and 24 the story is told of Lemech questioning Adam in regards to whether or not he and his wife should have additional children, in view of the impending flood. Adam responds, "Do your duty and begat", whereupon Lamech responds, "Physician, heal thyself," or

"Physician, cure your own lameness." The story continues that Adam then heeds Lamech's reproach and continues to beget children.

"Physician, heal thyself" is reminiscent of another saying, "Charity begins at home." The idea seems to be, *"You have been able to do miracles in Capernaum, now do some miracles here in your own home."* Of course the request was spoken in unbelief, as they knew Him only as Joseph's son. Therefore Jesus responds, *"A prophet is not without honor, except in his own country."*

It is also interesting to note here Jesus' use of the term "prophet" with reference to himself. This is obviously a pointed reference to the miracle-working ministry of the prophets Elijah and Elisha. Rejected in His own home, Jesus returns to Capernaum, where his devoted friends and believing disciples would gladly hear His word.

TEXT OR PRETEXT

QUESTION: Dear Dr. Blizzard: Could you please explain Acts 5:12-14? In verse 12, it says *"all the believers met together in Solomon's Colonnade."* In verse 13 it says, *"No one else dared join them, even though they were highly regarded by the people."* Then in verse 14, it states *"More and more believed and were added to their number."* If no one else dared join them, how were more added to their number?

ANSWER: It has been said that "A text taken out of context is pretext."

Notice that the context of this passage centers around the death of Ananias and Sapphira. This event brought great awe and fear of God to the Church. It had such a purifying influence that no one dared unite with this new movement for purely human reasons. However, the Church was held in high regard by the people and those who experienced a genuine spiritual transformation united with the Church, and there were a great number of such believers.

DOMINION THEOLOGY

QUESTION: Dear D. Blizzard: A question: I heard Dominion Theology back in the 1960's and I am beginning to hear it again. What heretic in early church history taught this nonsense? Was it Marcion?

ANSWER: Marcion's theology could not be likened, in the strictest sense, to the Dominion Theology of today, although they would share an idea or two in common. Marcion was a Gnostic and perhaps the most extreme and dangerous of his day. He taught that there were three primal forces, the good or gracious God that Christ made known, evil matter ruled by the devil, and the righteous world maker who is the finite, imperfect, angry Yehovah of the Jews. He was extremely anti-Jewish and taught that the God of the Old Testament is harsh, sever and unmerciful.

The Law, he taught, commanded you to love your neighbor and hate your enemy, and an eye-for-an-eye and a-tooth-for-a-tooth. The God of the New Testament commanded you to love your enemy. One, he said, is only just, the other good. He wrestled Jesus' words in Matthew 5:17 to read *"I am not come to fulfill the law and the prophets, but to destroy them."*

Christianity, he taught, fell abruptly and magically from heaven. Christ was not born but descended suddenly into the city of Capernaum in the 15th year of Tiberius and came to reveal the good God that had sent him. He had no connection with the Messiah of the Old Testament. His body was a mere appearance and his death an allusion.

Marcion was an ascetic in the strictest sense, abstaining from marriage, meat, and wine, and admitted married couples into his movement only after they had taken vows to abstain from all physical intercourse.

You may find it surprising to learn that the basic ideas promulgated in Dominion Theology, or the Kingdom Now movement, were actually proposed by Ignatius Loyola (1491-1566 C.E.) the founder of the Jesuit Order or, as they were also known, The Society of Jesus. Loyola demanded the crucifixion of the individual conscience in complete obedience to the authority of the Church. Their motto was, "all for the greater glory of God."

This meant to them the extension of the Kingdom upon earth. This kingdom was condensed in the Roman Church and represented by the Pope. All doctrines which deviated from the papal church were heresies. Those persons who deviated were considered emissaries of Satan whose influence had to be destroyed by any means. To accomplish their goals they formulated the doctrine of "intentionalism" which meant that "the end justified the means." The doctrine of "mental reservation" meant that man was not bound to state the whole truth on an oath. The doctrine of "probabilism" meant that the probability of a thing made it good. Personal responsibility to God and to truth was undermined by blind, unconditional obedience to authority. This movement became powerful almost at once.

In 1542, an institution called "The Holy Office" was established as a tribunal to discover and eradicate heresies. Those suspected were brought before this court and six cardinals were appointed as Inquisitors General with full powers of confiscation, imprisonment, banishment and death. The inquisition courts led to the Inquisition and nearly eradicated Protestantism.

It may come as something of a shock to learn that it is here that you find the true seeds of Reconstructionism and Dominion Theology.

References

KJV   King James Version of the Bible

NKJV   New King James Version of the Bible

CEB   Common English Bible

AMP   Amplified Bible

ISV   International Standard Version

ESV   English Standard Version

CJB   Complete Jewish Bible

ASV   American Standard Version

Brown, Driver Briggs

Everyman's Talmud

Mishnah

Printed in the United States
By Bookmasters